MURDER AT FEATHERS &
FLAIR

A GINGER GOLD MYSTERY

COPYRIGHT

THIS BOOK USES BRITISH SPELLING

CHAPTER ONE

"*Y*ou're a thief!"

The thief stepped forwards and replied, "Exactly. And you, madam? The mistress of the house, I presume. Or are you a thief as well?"

With a white-gloved hand Ginger Gold held the programme up in the dim light of the Abbott Theatre, an older establishment on Shaftesbury Avenue.

The thief was played by Angus Green, a handsome man, tall with a confidence that radiated from the stage. Ginger doubted his aplomb was only attributed to acting. He was young and had a determination about him. Probably new to theatre, Ginger thought—she hadn't heard his name before.

The one-act play written by a Mr. Stuart Walker was called *Sham*, and Ginger's sister-in-law, Felicia, had landed the lead female role of Clara.

"What have you taken?" Felicia's enunciation was loud and with proper indignation. "Give it to me instantly!

How dare you?" She gestured to the actor standing next to her. "Charles, take it away from him."

Haley Higgins, Ginger's American friend and house-mate, leaned in and whispered in her Bostonian accent, "Felicia has pluck."

Ginger agreed. On the stage *and* in real life, if truth be told.

Charles, according to the programme, was played by a blond man named Geordie Atkins. He was shorter and stouter than the attractive thief and a good deal older if you could go by his receding hairline.

"I dare say, old man," Geordie Atkins said, looking uncertain yet a little amused. "You'd better clear out."

Ambrosia, the Dowager Lady Gold and Ginger's grandmother through marriage, had not been a great supporter of her granddaughter's interest in theatre. "A lot of simpletons looking to escape their responsibilities," she'd stated. Yet, in the light filtering off the stage to their seats on the balcony, Ginger saw a smile and a glint in the older lady's eye she'd almost say was pride.

There were only four characters in the play—the fourth was a reporter who appeared near the end. A man in his early thirties donning a moustache and spectacles had won the part. He wore a trilby hat and an overcoat that hung sloppily over drooped shoulders. Ginger examined her programme: Matthew Haines. Felicia had talked about her fellow actors often since joining the company, and Ginger was glad to put names to faces.

In the end, Felicia's character conned the confidence man. When the curtain dropped, Ginger sprung to her feet in applause.

"Bravo! Bravo!"

The actors waited in the lobby to greet the members of the audience, who Ginger thought solemnly, were far too few. A jolly good number of seats had been unoccupied. Quite a shame since the performance was so charming.

"Felicia, darling!" Ginger said as she embraced her sister-in-law. "You were absolutely magnificent!"

Felicia had changed into a Jean Patou chiffon evening gown from Feathers & Flair. It had three layers of fabric each a different shade of pink, and a dropped waist cummerbund-like sash. Felicia's dark hair was perfectly coiffed with finger waves and decorated with a jewelled headpiece. The pink on her Clara Bow lips matched her dress. Ginger thought she rivalled any film star she'd ever seen.

Felicia held Ginger's green-eyed gaze. "Thank you, Ginger! I'm so glad you came."

A wayward strand of red hair escaped from Ginger's bob. When she pushed it behind her ear, her dangling Cartier Paris emerald and diamond earrings swayed. She gushed, "Wouldn't have missed it for the world."

Ambrosia allowed a quick hug from Felicia and begrudgingly admitted, "It was better than I expected, child. I do hope you have this folly out of your system now."

Felicia's smile lit up the lobby. "Oh, Grandmama! I'm so happy, even *you* cannot steal my joy tonight."

Haley shook Felicia's hand with a firm grip and said, "Good job, Felicia. Well done."

Felicia introduced her fellow actors, Mr. Geordie Atkins and Mr. Matthew Haines, but her gaze and smile stayed on the man who played the thief. "And this is Mr. Angus Green."

Angus shook each lady's hand as he charmed Ambrosia and showered Ginger with accolades.

"It's such an honour to meet you, Lady Gold. Felicia has told me so many great things."

Ginger arched a brow. "Is that so, Mr. Green?"

"Indeed. I hear you've started your own business! Very commendable. And that a rather prestigious gala is coming up."

Ginger laughed. "The rumours are true. Shall you be attending?"

Angus Green's dark eyes gazed down at Felicia. "If I'm invited."

Felicia beamed and threaded her fingers through his. "You know I've already invited you, silly." They laughed, and Ginger and Haley shared a look. Felicia was clearly smitten by her colleague.

Tapping her walking stick on the burgundy theatre carpet, Ambrosia's frown deepened, and her eyes narrowed at the public display of affection. Felicia had the sense to remove her hand from Mr. Green's.

"Let's move along, Grandmother," Ginger said before a displeasing scene could erupt. "We are holding up the queue."

THE NEXT DAY, Ginger's chauffeur Clement, a quiet, easy-going, middle-aged man from Yorkshire, drove Ginger to her Regent Street shop. The old 1913 Daimler TE 30 was in great shape, not having been driven much during the previous decade.

Though Ginger preferred to drive the motorcar herself, the bright side was she didn't have to worry about parking or having to dodge puddles in the street. This was especially good news for Boss, Ginger's black and white Boston Terrier, who sat eagerly on Ginger's lap. Instead, she could hop directly onto the pavement by the front entrance of Feathers & Flair.

"Thank you, Clement," Ginger said as she opened the kerbside door.

"You're welcome, madam. When should I collect you?"

"I'm not sure. I'll ring the house when I'm ready."

"Very well."

The Daimler puttered away, and Ginger strutted to the shop, one arm holding Boss and the other on her hat as she bore down against the wind.

A short line clogged up the entrance.

"I'm so sorry," Ginger said. "Please excuse me. I'm the proprietress here."

"Oh, Lady Gold!" a lady gushed. "I'm so excited to visit your shop. It's the talk of the fashion district!"

"Thank you. You're so kind."

Ginger manoeuvred past the small crowd and made way for a few shoppers to exit. She was happy to see smiles on the women's faces and large shopping bags in their hands. The patient customers who'd been waiting outside scurried in from the cold.

On seeing Ginger, Madame Roux hurried to her side. The manager wore a sensible but fashionable suit of lavender rayon. Her dark eyes, crinkling with deep crow's feet at the corners, flashed with excitement. "*Incroyable*! Word of the gala has spread like feathers from a torn pillow!"

"This is a good problem to have, Madame Roux," Ginger said.

Feathers & Flair had recently expanded to the second level of the stone building when the previous owner, a shoemaker, had retired and closed his shop. Both floors had ten-foot high creamy white ceilings with edgings painted gold. The floors consisted of polished white marble tiles which glistened under the bright electric crystal lamps. A rich burgundy velvet curtain hung over the archway that divided the front room from the back area.

Before setting Boss on the floor, Ginger wiped his paws with the cotton cloth she carried for this purpose. "To your bed, Bossy," she instructed. Boss immediately headed to the velvet curtain, pushed his nose through the seam in the middle, and disappeared.

Ginger handed Madame Roux her coat and handbag and headed up the wooden stairwell. The factory-made dresses, located on the upper floor, were always inspected —especially this latest shipment that had arrived for the gala. Several younger patrons clucked over the choices and tried on dresses for size.

"I love not having to wait for something to be made," one of them said.

Her companion added, "And these prices won't break the bank."

Dorothy West, the young floor clerk, moved about with quick strides, her mouth pinched in a tight line.

"Dorothy," Ginger whispered lightly, "do remember to smile."

The girl's head snapped towards Ginger's voice, staring like a nervous bird. The muscles around her small mouth twitched before straining upward. "Yes, Lady Gold. I'm just a tad nervous. Most of the high society ladies I know aren't as nice as you, madam."

Ginger herself had trouble with the entitlement of the elite. She smiled her encouragement. "You'll be fine. Everyone will mellow after drinking his or her first glass of champagne. At least that's what I'm counting on."

The muscles in Dorothy's face relaxed. "Thank you, madam."

The main floor, where the haute couture designs were displayed, showed the latest samples from all the prestigious fashion houses, both in Europe and America. Ginger admired a new frock—golden sheer over a solid gold chemise. The sheer was stitched with glittery sequins and shiny thread work in Egyptian-inspired designs and hung four inches lower than the chemise underneath to mid-calf. Egyptian themes had become popular in fashion and design since Howard Carter's discovery of King Tutankhamen's tomb in '22, and Ginger was jolly keen about them all.

Ginger's young designer, Emma Miller, brought more dresses out from the back room to refit the mannequins. She had a ready smile and seemed to sincerely enjoy her job.

"I've worked on some new designs," she said when she saw Ginger. "I've sketched them on the easel."

"I'll have a look." Ginger admired the young girl's

eagerness to please and saw real potential in her ideas. Emma Miller could be a big name one day, and Ginger loved that she could be a part of the designer's success.

A sophisticated lady in a lamb's wool cape admired the latest frocks in from New York.

"Lady Whitmore," Ginger said, recognising her. "Welcome to Feathers & Flair."

"Thank you, Lady Gold. It's not my first time in, you know." The lady leaned in conspiratorially. "Is it true Mr. Edward Molyneux is to be your guest at the opening gala?"

Ginger smiled broadly. When she'd invited the famous London-born designer, she could only dream that he'd agree to leave his shop in Paris to be her guest. Not only that, he promised to reveal one of his most recent designs at the gala.

"Yes, it is. I'm very excited to have him here."

"It's all the talk in the society pages, even though one wouldn't imagine such an event to be held in a dressmaker's shop."

"We're not a dressmaker's shop, Lady Whitmore," Ginger defended. "We're a dress shop where the finest fashions of the world can be found. It makes sense that a gala to promote them would happen here."

"Yes, of course. I completely agree. I'm just repeating what I've heard."

Ginger smiled stiffly. She had little patience for gossipers.

Lady Whitmore patted Ginger on the arm. "Word is that royals from all over Europe are coming to London to shop for their spring wardrobe, and especially to see your shop, so don't you spend one minute worrying about those naysayers' rumours. Your supply is magnificent, by the way. You know the other shops are up in arms, don't you? You've become major competition and in such a short time. Don't be surprised if they send spies in as pretend shoppers. After all, the owners wouldn't dare to enter. Imagine what people would say?"

Ginger left Lady Whitmore to browse, and soon the loquacious lady found another willing to listen to her tittle-tattle. Madame Roux approached Ginger with a customer at her side. The client wore a tan-coloured wool coat that Ginger recognised as one of Parisian designer Jean Lanvin's collection. Tall for a lady, the customer stood straight with the best posture finishing school could produce, despite her bountiful bosom which was bound to weight the lady forward. Her ample bottom accounted for a slight waddle when she walked. She wasn't what one would call handsome, yet the lady had a familiar look about her. A straight nose, small chin, and grey eyes, heavily made up with blue shadow and thick mascara. Her lips were a glossy red.

"This is Countess Andreea Balcescu from Romania," Madame Roux said. "This is Lady Gold, the owner of Feathers & Flair."

Ginger held out a gloved hand. "How do you do, Countess Balcescu. And welcome!"

The countess did not have an easy smile. Most of the aristocracy from the East were suffering from the war's aftermath. Many were refugees of revolutions, and some-times, their family lineage had legally and abruptly ended.

"I have heard grand things about your shop," the

countess said, her husky voice hinting at a slight accent. "I have had to leave many of my possessions behind and have great hope to replenish my spring wardrobe in London."

"I'd most certainly be happy to help you with that. We have the latest fashions shipped in from Paris and New York and have our own fabulous designer in-house. We can produce a unique gown to your liking."

"That is impressive."

Ginger presented a turquoise and silver evening gown with fascinating silver embellishments draped over the bodice and light chiffon cap-sleeves. She watched as Countess Balcescu ran her fingers across the dress. Her gloved hands were large but handled the fabric delicately.

Behind them, a display of accessories crashed to the floor making everyone jump.

"*Mon Dieu*," Madame Roux exclaimed. Dorothy and Emma hurried to set the display upright and replaced the handbags and scarves.

"How did that happen?" Ginger asked.

"I have no idea," Madame Roux said. "It's so crowded, anyone could have bumped it over."

Or pushed it over. Ginger was reminded of Lady Whitmore's warning of the other shops sending over spies. Would someone deliberately try to sabotage her event?

That was nonsense talking. The falling display was a mere accident.

The countess wasn't impressed. "Perhaps I will return another time when things are less . . . hectic."

Ginger sighed. There went a potential customer, most

likely to one of her competitors. Oh well. Couldn't be helped. These things happened.

The telephone bell rang intermittently with Madame Roux managing the calls, but this time, her manager caught her attention and waved her over.

"The telephone is for you, Lady Gold. It's Miss Gold."

Ginger took the receiver. Unlike the older candlestick version installed at Hartigan House, this one was a modern machine with the earpiece and receiver in one which, when not in use, rested horizontally over a boxy unit with a circular dial.

"Felicia?"

"Oh, Ginger. I think something horrible has happened."

Ginger's heart skipped a beat. Had something happened at home? Was Ambrosia all right? The matronly lady had a lot of tenacity, but she wasn't getting any younger. "What is it?"

"Angus Green has gone missing!"

Ginger blinked at the news. Not at all what she was expecting. Angus Green—the handsome young actor Felicia was soft on? "What do you mean he's missing?"

"He didn't show up for rehearsal this afternoon and Geordie Atkins says he didn't come home at all last night. They share a flat, you see."

"Perhaps he tired of the theatre and left to do something new?"

"I don't think he would do that. There are still two nights of the show remaining. He wouldn't leave us high and dry, would he? Besides, he promised me we'd celebrate together when it ended."

Felicia's voice caught, and Ginger felt a wave of sympathy. "Are there any indications of foul play?"

"Geordie said his room had been roughed up. Apparently Angus is a tidy type of fellow. And now that I think of it, he had seemed rather tense these last few days, like he had something on his mind."

"Have you called the police?"

"Yes, but they're not taking us seriously. They think Mr. Green is just a wild sort, doing his own thing. Ginger, you have to find him."

"Me?"

"Mr. Haines is moneyed. He says he'll pay you."

Ginger sputtered, "I'm not a private investigator, Felicia."

"But you are! You've solved so many mysteries since coming to England. Please Ginger, take the case."

Ginger gaped at her sister-in-law's plea.

Oh, mercy.

CHAPTER TWO

*M*aking her excuses to Madame Roux, Ginger—with Boss under one arm—stepped outside in search of a taxicab. Felicia had agreed to meet her at the Abbott Theatre. Ginger had never taken on a missing person's case before, and already regretted agreeing to take this one. She wasn't qualified and had no idea where to even start, but thought a quick interview of Angus Green's fellow actors and stage mates wouldn't hurt.

Ginger hailed a black Beardmore taxicab that had a covered carriage and large wings over spoked tyres.

"You don't mind my dog?" she asked.

The driver shrugged. "So long as it doesn't make a mess."

Ginger placed Boss on the leather seat then sorted her long winter coat around her legs as she slipped in beside him. Underneath, she wore a blue flat-crepe dress trimmed with silver braiding and a hemline that offended Ambrosia, with its trim just below the knee.

"The Abbott Theatre, please," she instructed.

"Certainly, madam."

January in England was usually damp and grey, and this January day was no different. A fog had settled over the city making visibility a challenge for all those who navigated Oxford Street toward the theatre district—motorcars, horses and carriages, and daring cyclists. The taxicab driver squeezed the ball of his horn every few minutes.

When they finally arrived at the theatre, Ginger clipped Boss's leash to his collar, paid the driver, and hurried inside. What remained of the cast of *Sham* was assembled on the stage. Lit only by the electric lamps high up on the wall and some stage lighting, the theatre was dark.

Felicia rushed to greet Ginger and ushered her through the doors on stage right. The perspective from the stage differed from Ginger's earlier view from her box seat the evening before. An empty orchestra pit gaped in front, dark and dangerous, should someone fall in. Just beyond that, the seats tiered up in a steep incline like a red-velvet cliff.

Mr. Atkins, Mr. Haines, and a man Ginger had never met, sat on foldable wooden chairs. Ginger put the stranger in his late forties, a studious sort with slicked-back hair and a waxed moustache. He greeted Ginger with a firm handshake.

"I'm Peter Maguire, stage manager."

"How do you do, Mr. Maguire?"

He gave Boss a disapproving look before saying, "I hope you don't mind meeting us here. I just thought it would be the most central and also the most private." He clicked his tongue. "This situation is odious. I'll have to *cancel* the show because of that bounder."

The stage manager obviously didn't believe harm had come to Mr. Green if his concern was for the show. Geordie Atkins ran a hand through his thinning hair and exhaled a defeated breath. He stood when Ginger drew closer. "Thanks for coming," was all he said.

Matthew Haines shuffled to his feet, shoulders hunched, and shook Ginger's hand. He was slender and fine-boned, and his palm felt distinctly narrow and soft. Acting didn't rough up a man's hands as physical labour would. He wore a forest-green wool-knit winter sweater —a fashion made popular by the Prince of Wales—over a white cotton shirt and brown trousers. "Nice to see you again, Lady Gold. So sorry it's under these strange circumstances."

"Do you really believe Mr. Green is in some kind of danger or has suffered a mishap?" Ginger asked. "Is this sort of behaviour out of character for him?"

"I don't know if Angus is in harm's way or not," Geordie said. "But you can be sure that disappearing without a word is not something he'd do unless circumstances merited it."

Peter Maguire played with his moustache as he nodded in agreement. "Angus is a serious lad who's intent on becoming a successful actor. He planned to leave for New York this summer."

Felicia's eyes grew wide at the news. Clearly Angus hadn't been completely forthcoming.

"Who was the last to see him?" Ginger asked.

"I believe that was me," Felicia said softly. "We went out for drinks after the show last night. He brought me home after midnight, I believe. Wanting to be refreshed for today's rehearsal, he was going to his flat straightaway. At least, that's what he told me."

Mr. Maguire clucked his tongue again and repeated, "I'll have to cancel the last two shows. We don't train an understudy for short performances like these. "

"Oh, Mr. Maguire," Felicia said. "I'm so disappointed. Angus is not going to hear the last of it from me once he's found!"

"Perhaps I should see his flat," Ginger said. Geordie dug into his pocket and produced a set of keys. "I'll drive you."

GEORDIE ATKINS and Angus Green's flat was in the City of London just beyond the imposing structure of St. Paul's Cathedral and not far from St. George's Anglican Church. From the sitting room window looking south toward the Thames, Ginger could see the square, castle-like turret that overwhelmed the rest of the stone church. If she'd driven the Daimler, she would've stopped in to see Reverend Oliver Hill and check in on their Child Wellness Project, a charity that aided the hungry street children.

The actors' flat was sparsely decorated with a lone sofa and coffee table in the living room, a wooden table and two chairs in the kitchen.

Ginger commanded Boss to sit by the door and then scanned the flat.

Geordie watched her take it in. "We like to travel light. You never know where the next show is going to take us."

The bathroom had a white claw-foot tub—its enamel cracking—a small sink and the toilet. The mirror of the medicine cabinet stood open, and Ginger examined the contents. "Does anything in here belong to Mr. Green?"

Geordie nodded. "He has the bottom shelf. That's his toothbrush, his shaving cream and those powders are his medicament packets."

Ginger doubted Angus Green would leave, no matter how short the notice, without his private toiletries. She turned to Geordie. "Is it possible Mr. Green left involuntarily?"

"What do you mean?"

"Did he have any enemies?"

Geordie shrugged. "Honestly, I don't know the bloke all that well."

"As of late, did his behaviour seem odd?"

"He did seem out of sorts. Worried about something, I'd wager." Geordie shrugged again. "But, in this business, Lady Gold, nothing is ever what it seems."

CHAPTER THREE

$\mathcal{T}$he 1924 gala event at Feathers & Flair *was* the talk of London. Everyone who was anyone in polite society was there, and even a few who weren't so polite, such as the Daily News reporter, Blake Brown. He stood nearly eye-to-eye with Ginger who was wearing silver silk brocade two-inch heels. His thin hair was heavily oiled and parted on the side. His small brown eyes looked bored. A leather-covered Swiss-made Sico camera was strapped over the shoulder of his suit jacket, which bulged over a round belly.

"You certainly know how to throw a party, Lady Gold," he said. "If I remember correctly, your last blast was a 'dead' one." He chuckled at his own *double entendre*.

"Oh, Mr. Brown," Ginger said with distaste. "Please don't bring that up. I can assure you that no one is going to die tonight."

"I was only pulling your leg."

She eyed him sideways. "I'm surprised to see you. This isn't the kind of thing you normally cover, is it?"

"My editor insisted." Blake Brown shrugged. "Free booze. It was the best offer I had tonight."

A waiter passed by with drinks on a tray. Brown emptied his glass in a quick swig and grabbed another. Ginger was tempted to slap the man's hand away but instead smiled like a good hostess should.

"If you'll excuse me," she said without awaiting a response.

The girls had done an utterly fabulous job decorating. There were bouquets of white and gold helium-filled balloons, large bouquets of white roses in crystal vases, and silk ribbons hanging from the ceiling. White-gloved waiters dressed in black suits slid between the patrons, balancing trays of champagne-filled flute glasses. In one corner, a jazz singer crooned popular tunes.

Ginger passed the Fitzhugh mother and daughter duo, regulars at Feathers & Flair.

"Good heavens, Meredith. Stand up straight!" Lady Fitzhugh demanded. She was certainly hard on her daughter, Ginger thought.

The poor girl pouted and threw her doughy shoulders back. Lady Meredith hadn't been blessed with good looks —her face too wide and her mouth too small—and an overbearing mother only added to the young lady's blatant lack of confidence.

"Lady Fitzhugh, Lady Meredith, such a pleasure to see you both." Ginger offered a smile.

"These kinds of parties aren't really for me, but I thought it might be good for Meredith." Lady Fitzhugh clucked. "I'd hoped for more young men to be present."

"Mother, please!" Meredith's puffy face flushed red with mortification.

Ginger tried to make light of the older lady's insensitivity. "My shop appeals mainly to women, so I'm afraid the men are quite outnumbered. I hope you do enjoy yourselves, regardless."

Beyond the Fitzhughs, Ginger spotted Princess Sophia von Altenhofen from Berlin. Shopping for her spring wardrobe, Ginger hoped. She recognised the royal from a feature she'd read in the *Gazette du Bon Ton*, an influential French fashion magazine. It was an article from before the war, but the princess had changed little over the years.

"Princess von Altenhofen." Ginger greeted her formally, knowing that the new republic in Germany had abolished the status of nobility. Their titles were nothing more than an extension of their names.

"I hope you enjoy the music," Ginger said. "Do you like jazz?"

"Yes, the new music is soothing, but I have not come for comfort. I have come to meet Herr Molyneux."

"Of course. He shall be joining us shortly."

In the back room with his assistant, Mr. Edward Molyneux was making last minute adjustments to his presentation. A tumbler of whisky sat on the small table next to his chair. He wanted to create anticipation, he said when asked why he refused to mingle.

Lady Isla Lyon and her husband, Lord Robert Lyon, were chatting with Lord and Lady Whitmore. Lord Whitmore, a pinkish man with wiry, straw-coloured hair, towered over his wife and the other couple, his gaze discreetly roaming the room. Unlike most people, Ginger knew Lord Whitmore was with the secret service. When their eyes met, he nodded imperceptibly.

Countess Andreea Balcescu had shown up for the gala as promised, and Ginger crossed the room to greet her. The countess wore a glamorous midnight-blue, sequin-studded rayon gown that dropped in a straight line from her chest. Unfortunately for her, no amount of binding could bring about the desired boyish look that was currently in fashion.

"Countess! So good of you to come."

"Monsieur Molyneux is not to be missed."

Ginger smiled. "I agree!"

Haley saluted Ginger when she joined them. "Nicely done," she said with a smile and toasted her friend with a glass of champagne.

A lady Ginger had never seen before, petite with shiny dark hair and salon-perfect Marcel waves cascading from the top of her head to her delicate chin, approached with confidence, her bejewelled hand extended.

"Lady Gold, I'm Mrs. Emelia Reed. It's such a pleasure to finally meet. My husband speaks very highly of you."

The well-dressed man beside her turned and Ginger felt the floor shift underneath her. "Basil?"

Ginger had met Chief Inspector Basil Reed the previous summer aboard the SS *Rosa*. There had been an immediate attraction between them which they both resisted. He claimed he was in a troubled marriage destined for divorce, and she was still privately mourning the death of her husband, even though he'd been gone for five years.

Basil had begrudgingly allowed her to help in solving a

crime that had happened aboard ship—Ginger could be quite persuasive when she wanted—and they parted ways having gained each other's respect.

As it turned out, crime continued to bring them together and a proper friendship developed. Her feelings had grown more serious than mere friendship, so much so that she'd put away the photo of Daniel that had sat on her bedside table since the war. It was a tearful goodbye to her first love, but Ginger knew Daniel would want her to be happy and move on. As Daniel was prone to say during the war, "The living have to keep on living."

Ginger had never confessed her feelings to the chief inspector, but she was certain he was aware of them. Basil Reed knew how to read people. It was one thing that made him good at his job. Ginger thought she was good at reading people too. She had been sure Basil's feelings for her went beyond friendship.

Apparently she'd been wrong.

"Hello, Lady Gold." Basil's hazel eyes held hers, apologetically. "My wife decided she wished to attend at the last minute. We didn't have a chance to RSVP."

RSVPs weren't required. Basil was telling her he hadn't had a chance to warn her, to let her know his wife had returned.

Trained during the war to keep her emotions hidden, Ginger responded as expected under the most extreme and stressful of circumstances—no matter what was at stake. In the war years, her life had depended on it.

Now, her personal dignity did.

"Pleased to meet you, Mrs. Reed." Ginger pasted on a smile though it felt as if her blood had drained to her feet.

"Basil says you're very good at details and management, Lady Gold." Emelia Reed waved her free hand. "Clearly you have a head for business."

Ginger responded with false gaiety, "Thank you." She caught Basil's eye. "Perhaps I could outfit you with something."

He ducked his smoothly shaven chin. "I think I'll stick to Savile Row."

Savile Row was the area of London where the male species of polite society shopped for fine garments. Not, strictly speaking, a competitor to Feathers & Flair.

Emelia Reed stroked Basil's waistcoat and patted him affectionately. "I think Savile Row is the only place for you, darling." She held Ginger's gaze. "My husband looks smashing. Don't you agree?"

"I do, Mrs. Reed," Ginger answered lightly. Were Felicia watching, she'd be astounded at Ginger's acting skills. "I hope you both will enjoy the evening."

"I'm sure we will," Emelia Reed said. "I've been out of town for some time." She threaded her fingers through her husband's hand and beamed up at Basil. Ginger was quite certain the display was for her benefit. Emelia Reed arched a dark, well-defined brow. "It's good to get back into the swing of things."

"Of course," Ginger said politely. Though tears burned at the back of her eyes, she fought to control them. She mustn't show improper emotion. Basil hadn't promised her anything, hadn't done anything wrong. She'd made foolish assumptions. This new pain in her chest was her own fault.

"Nice to see you again, Chief Inspector," Ginger said

with false brightness. She spun away and headed for the back room. A tear escaped even as she felt Basil's gaze burn a hole through her back. She flung the dividing curtain apart with more strength than necessary.

"Mr. Molyneux."

The designer had an authoritative way about him and looked well put together in an exquisitely tailored black dinner jacket. His brown hair was combed back from a pleasant-looking face.

"Are you quite ready?" Ginger asked.

He stood straight and tugged on his lapels. "We are indeed."

The designer's assistant, Mademoiselle Bernard, jumped to attention. "The displays are set," she said.

Edward Molyneux smiled at Ginger. "I'm ready. You may introduce me."

His accent had taken on a definite French lilt, which made Ginger smile. Though the designer's fashion house was on a much-desired street in Paris, he had, in fact, been born in London. Ginger agreed the French persona was more persuasive.

Ginger slipped through the dividing curtain to face her guests. She deliberately did *not* look at Basil Reed.

CHAPTER FOUR

"*L*adies and gentlemen, allow me to present Monsieur Molyneux!"

Mr. Molyneux passed through the curtain with a swagger, and the guests applauded with sincere appreciation. He entranced the crowd as Mademoiselle Bernard wheeled out sketches of Molyneux's latest designs followed by the grand finale of three mannequins dressed in never-seen-before gowns. Molyneux's designs were modern with strong lines and limited decoration, and the exposed back and shoulders had, in the past, led some to call his dresses outrageous.

Ginger was happy to note that her guests didn't appear to be among those. An appreciative chorus rang out.

"Fabulous!"

"Outstanding!"

"Simply divine!"

Lady Whitmore declared loudly to her husband. "A fashionable lady turns to his designs if she wants to be absolutely right without being utterly predictable."

"When can we make a purchase?" a voice called out.

Ginger smiled. "The register shall open at ten p.m. Please do browse until then. My staff is eager to be of assistance."

The front entrance opened letting in a waft of much-appreciated cool air. An unbelievably gorgeous lady—perhaps the most beautiful that Ginger had ever seen—walked in, causing the room to still. She entered as if she didn't notice the effect her presence created. Her gown, a stunning, creamy chiffon with three layers that flowed below the knee. An Egyptian Assiut tulle shawl, with hammered silver pieces that created the design, fell over slender shoulders. Sitting delicately against the creamy white of her skin, a large teardrop-cut blue diamond hung from a simple silver chain. Its presence precipitated a collective intake of breath. Ginger recognised the gem from a piece she'd read in the Boston Herald. The *Blue Desire* was priceless and believed to be unlucky. Apparently, all its previous owners had fallen into bad times and ultimately lost the diamond one way or another. Many had even lost their lives while in possession of the breath-taking gem. There was a mythical quality about the blue diamond, especially with how the electric lights caused it to sparkle, that made Ginger believe one could be rendered helpless in one's desire to own it.

The sophisticated lady scoured the room with her midnight eyes until they found Ginger. Like a sleek panther, the lady crossed the marble floor. "You must be Lady Gold, the owner of this fine establishment." Her melodious voice had a hint of a Russian accent. "I am Grand Duchess Olga Pavlovna Orlova."

Ginger wasn't sure about the protocol. Her eyes darted to Haley who shrugged. Ginger reached out her hand. "How do you do, Grand Duchess? Welcome to Feathers & Flair."

"Thank you. It is my greatest joy to be here. The English are my new family as I'm no longer welcome in my own country."

"I'm very sorry to hear about your hardships. I hope you will find rest and comfort in England."

"As do I."

The crowd relaxed and returned to their own conversations. Lady Fitzhugh's voice grew louder with each champagne refill. "If only you'd have turned out like that, Meredith."

Meredith's small mouth tightened into a knot. She glared at her mother before shooting hot daggers at Olga Pavlovna.

Oh, mercy. Ginger felt sorry for Lady Meredith.

Princess von Altenhofen moved beside the Fitzhughs. "Don't listen to her," she said to Meredith. "The grand duchess is not what she seems." The princess moved on to speak to the guest of honour. Ginger marvelled at the conversation. What had the princess meant by that?

Felicia approached, her heart-shaped face long with melancholy. "Ginger, I hope you don't mind if I leave early. It's simply too hard to be here without Angus. Not knowing if he's safe or not is dreadful."

"I understand, love," Ginger said, feeling a mite remorseful at not giving Angus Green more of her attention. Once this gala was over, she'd focus on nothing else.

"Go home and rest. Do remember to check on Grandmother."

Claiming a headache, Ambrosia had declined the invitation to the gala. Ginger allowed that late nights and crowds could be too much for the older lady's nerves.

Princess von Altenhofen had Edward Molyneux cornered. In her distinctively German accent, she asked if she could make a private appointment.

"It would be my delight to create something specifically for you, Princess von Altenhofen."

"*Vielen Dank.*" The princess had her back to the room— apparently the only one uninterested in the Russian grand duchess. Though 'polite' society returned to 'polite' conversation, the darting of eyes made it quite clear the grand duchess had captured everyone's interest.

The Russian goddess caused an unfamiliar sense of inadequacy to jolt through Ginger. Having just been rejected by Basil Reed certainly didn't help.

With a royal air the grand duchess strolled to where the fashion designer and German princess stood and deftly interrupted. Princess Sophia's look of disdain was undeniable. She clearly didn't like the grand duchess, and after thanking Molyneux a second time she stormed off.

The grand duchess remained unruffled. "The Germans don't like coming in second, do they?"

Mr. Molyneux had the good sense to remain neutral. "I'm thankful that the war is over and we can all focus on life and joy, such as my designs bring."

"The war is over for you, monsieur, but in my country, the suffering continues."

"Indeed. Forgive my insensitivity."

"No need to apologise. You are not a Bolshevik."

"Is there a dress of mine that interests you?" he asked.

Before Ginger could overhear the princess' answer, her attention was drawn to Madame Roux's loud cry behind her. "Lady Whitmore!"

Ginger turned in time to see Madame Roux propping up Lady Whitmore and rushed to the lady's side.

"Lady Whitmore?"

The lady's eyelashes fluttered as she regained her strength and returned her weight to her own two feet.

"I'm sorry, I don't know what happened there."

"Would you like to sit down?" Ginger said. "There's an empty chair right over there."

Lady Whitmore nodded and with Madame Roux's help, she led the lady to a chair.

"I'll get you some water," Madame Roux said.

Lord Whitmore leaned over his wife. "Sara?"

"I'm afraid I don't feel well. I hate to leave, but I do believe I need to be taken home before I cause a greater scene."

Lady Whitmore did look rather green, Ginger thought. She really must be ill to allow herself to become the object of gossip, as she most definitely had.

Lord Whitmore's expression grew serious and he looked a bit stunned by the turn of events. "Drink a glass of water," he said. "Perhaps you'll feel better then."

"I'm truly not well."

"It's a little early to leave, don't you think. We'll make a scene."

"If I collapse on the floor, that won't make a scene?"

Ginger watched the interaction with curiosity. Most

men would give their right arm for an excuse to leave an event so geared toward the softer sex.

Lady Whitmore tugged on her husband's sleeve. "George, please."

He snorted through his nostrils, resigned. "Of course."

"I've asked Madame Roux to ring a taxicab," Ginger said as she stepped closer. "I know your driver might be hard to reach at short notice."

Lord Whitmore tucked his chin in thanks. Madame Roux arrived with Lady Whitmore's coat and the taxicab was already outside by the time they stepped onto the pavement.

With that crisis over, the patrons returned to their tight circles to continue chatting. Ginger couldn't stop herself from seeking out Basil's wife and found her laughing with Lady Lyon.

What on earth could they be talking about? It wasn't Ginger's business and she knew it. She accepted a flute of champagne from a passing waiter and approached Mr. Molyneux who for a rare moment was left standing alone.

"Mr. Molyneux! The gala is a success in part because you agreed to come. I can't thank you enough."

Mr. Molyneux smiled politely.

"It is I who should thank you, Lady Gold. I intend to open a shop in London one day, and this has given me much-needed publicity." He cocked his head. "We are to be rivals, I suppose."

Ginger laughed. "Competition is good for democracy."

"And democracy is good?"

"It is."

"How sad our neighbours to the east don't seem to agree."

Ginger nodded, her eyes landing on the Russian grand duchess. The lady never smiled; her sadness evident in her deep blue eyes. Ginger could only imagine the suffering she and her family must have gone through. Imagine being forced to flee one's own country. The aristocrats in Moscow and Petrograd were wise not to risk the same horrible fate the Tsar and his family had endured—all seven, executed together.

Ginger glanced away in time to see another member of the female aristocracy collapse. Princess Sophia von Altenhofen slumped onto the drinks table, causing a decanter of sherry to tip and fall. Thankfully, it was nearly empty, and its contents didn't spray onto the elegant dresses nearby.

Olga Pavlovna muttered in Russian.

"Princess Sophia," Ginger said, coming to her aid. "Are you all right?"

"I do not know what has come over me. Perhaps I've had one champagne too many."

Ginger nodded to Madame Roux, "Please open the door for a few minutes to freshen the air. Not too long, mind."

Countess Balcescu's habit of clicking her tongue went into gear. "None have the constitution we have in Romania. We would not think of fainting in front of our peers."

Ginger did think it rather odd that two women had succumbed to the vapours. She recalled Lady Whitmore's word of warning. Were there spies from her competition in the room, sabotaging the event? She frowned at Blake

Brown as he scribbled in his notepad. This was *not* the press she'd been hoping for.

Later when calm was restored, Ginger approached the journalist with a peace offering, the last of the brandy in a cut-glass tumbler in her hand.

"I do hope you'll be kind," she said as she held it out to him. He accepted the gift and sipped.

"I'll make light of the weaker women and focus on your designer guest. He's really the news item here."

"I thank you for your discretion. And please, no names."

Blake Brown chewed on his pencil. "I can't promise that. They *are* public figures, you know. But seeing as I don't normally do society pages, as a favour to you, Lady Gold, I think I can let their names slip my mind. However, if another lady goes down, all bets are off."

Oh, please, don't let there be a third one, Ginger thought. That would definitely shine the wrong kind of light on her opening.

The rest of the evening went without a hitch. The singer performed until eleven, which was when the drinks trolley was whisked away. Patrons left with their drivers, most with smiles on their faces. Ginger was satisfied the opening had gone well, and Madame Roux told her she had a list of new clients booked for fittings. Edward Molyneux had left earlier via taxicab, but his assistant remained behind to pack up the display dresses.

"It was a fabulous party, Lady Gold," Mademoiselle Bernard said excitedly. "I knew Monsieur Molyneux's new line would be a smashing success.

Once all the guests had gone, Madame Roux locked

the front door, leaving only the assistant, Ginger, Madame Roux, and Haley behind.

"Honey, I don't know how you do it," Haley said. "I'm exhausted from all the small talk."

"And you don't mind the little white lie?" Ginger asked carefully.

"That I was your rich American cousin?" Haley laughed. "Apparently, Felicia isn't the only actress living at Hartigan House. I've surprised myself with the yarns I created."

Madame Roux called out loudly from the back room. "Lady Gold!"

Ginger and Haley moved towards the anxious sound of the manager's voice and stopped short just inside the second changing area. A woman lay with her stomach on the floor.

"Another has fainted, madam?"

Ginger gaped at the lady's cream chiffon dress. There was no denying the owner. Her hand flew to her mouth.

"It's the grand duchess!"

Haley pulled up on her skirt and squatted to check for a pulse on the lady's neck. Ginger was glad Blake Brown wasn't around to take pictures.

The grand duchess' head lay at an unnatural angle. "Is she . . . dead?" Ginger asked.

Haley stared up grimly. "I'm afraid so."

CHAPTER FIVE

Ginger closed her eyes. How could this have happened?

Selfishly her mind focused on the hard work she had put into the gala which had now been ruined. Once Blake Brown got wind of this, Feathers & Flair would be famous for all the wrong reasons.

A lady's life had ended tonight. Ginger shook her head, reprimanding herself. She mustn't think of her own interests.

Light weeping caught Ginger's attention and she remembered Molyneux's young assistant. "Mademoiselle Bernard, you must not look," Ginger blurted. "There is a telephone at the desk. Call Scotland Yard. The number is in a blue book in the drawer."

Fortified now that she had something productive to do, the assistant wiped her eyes.

Madame Roux found her voice. "*Quelle horreur!* Whatever are we going to do?"

"We wait for the police," Ginger said.

Haley stood and nodded. "I'm sure a post-mortem will be required, since this is quite obviously a murder. The body is warm and hasn't started to rigor."

"I'm trying to remember the last time I saw her," Ginger said. "She was talking to Mr. Molyneux."

"I thought I saw her go upstairs," Madame Roux said. "She obviously came down again."

"I'm afraid I was focused on the entertainment most of the night," Haley said. "What time was it when you saw her talking to Mr. Molyneux?"

"Almost ten," Ginger said. "I remember because I announced the register would open in ten minutes."

Haley checked her wristwatch. "It's midnight right now. She's been dead for at least an hour, but less than two."

"How is it possible that no one noticed she was missing?" Ginger squatted next to Haley. "It seemed as if everyone had eyes on her."

"There must've been at least one moment when she slipped beyond the curtain unseen," Haley said. "Out of sight, out of mind."

"But what was she doing back here? What was she looking for?"

"Monsieur's designs?" Madame Roux suggested.

"We must ask Mademoiselle Bernard if anything is missing." Ginger left the crime scene and found Molyneux's assistant at the front desk staring into space.

"I know this is quite a shock," Ginger said. She poured a glass of water from the fountain and offered it to the girl. "Drink this."

Mademoiselle Bernard sipped it obediently.

"Have you contacted the police?" Ginger asked.

Mademoiselle Bernard nodded. "Oui."

"Good. Now I need you to think carefully. When you packed up this evening, was anything amiss? Was anything unaccounted for?"

Mademoiselle Bernard removed a hatpin from her hat, scratched her head, and replaced the hat. "I don't think so, Lady Gold. But I wasn't really thinking about it. I shall check."

Mademoiselle Bernard disappeared behind the curtain just as someone knocked on the front door.

Basil Reed stared back at Ginger through the glass. He removed the trilby from his head.

A thick wave of fatigue rolled over Ginger. The gala had expended all her reserves. The emotional weight of seeing Basil with his wife, and now a murder, left her with little energy to face the chief inspector. She let out a sigh and unlocked the door.

Ginger averted her eyes as Basil and Sergeant Scott, who hovered behind, stepped inside. Basil had changed into a sturdy brown suit, which showed through the opening of his trench coat.

"Ginger," he started, but before he could say anything that would embarrass them both, she interrupted. "Gentlemen. The body is in the third changing room at the back."

Ginger led them behind the curtain to where Haley and Madame Roux waited with the body.

Mademoiselle Bernard poked her head in. "Nothing's out of place, madam."

"It's late, Madame Roux," Ginger said. "Would you

assist Mademoiselle Bernard and help her to her hotel?" She glanced at Basil without looking into his eyes. "Is that okay, Chief Inspector?"

Basil nodded. "So long as neither of you leaves London. I'd like to ask a few questions tomorrow."

The women were quick to agree to the terms.

"Who was the last to see the grand duchess alive?" Basil asked.

"I saw her just before ten," Ginger said. "She was talking to Mr. Molyneux."

"I'll need to speak to the designer."

"He was one of the first to leave tonight."

Basil nodded. He had still been in the shop when Molyneux left.

"But Madame Roux said she saw the grand duchess go upstairs after he left, so Mr. Molyneux can't be implicated."

"Righto."

Basil jotted something in his notebook, then asked, "What's upstairs?"

"More clothes. Mostly factory made."

"Why would the grand duchess go up there?"

"I really don't know. She's not the type to be interested in factory frocks."

"Perhaps she met up with someone," Haley suggested.

"Can I have a look upstairs?" Basil asked. He obviously hadn't bothered with a tour during the gala.

"Certainly."

Unlike the lower floor, spare in its contents, the upper level had clothing racks lining from front to back along the hardwood floors. Clothing hung in like styles from sizes small to large. A rack of coats left over from last season had been priced for clearance. The new line of spring wear filled the rest, from casual blouses and skirts to day dresses, evening wear, and jackets. A local milliner provided Feathers & Flair with a selection of hats that hung on hooks on the wall.

"Did you notice anything unusual at the gala?" Basil asked. "Overhear a conversation that might point to bad blood with the grand duchess?"

"Well," Ginger started, "Princess Sophia von Altenhofen didn't hide her dislike of the lady."

Basil jotted something in his notebook. "Russian and German tensions are still high. Perhaps I can get a guest list from you."

"Of course."

Basil nodded and turned back to the steps. Suddenly he stopped and pivoted. Ginger nearly collided with him, only just keeping herself from having to touch him to retain her balance.

Basil stared at her without blinking. "Ginger, I'd like to explain."

Ginger took a small step back. She wasn't ready to face this right now. "Please, let's just keep to the case."

Basil sighed with resignation. "Very well."

Sergeant Scott had the Yard's new French Furet camera strapped around his neck and began taking photographs from every conceivable angle, nearly blinding Ginger as the flash lamps went off.

Basil saw her look of confusion. "Is something amiss?"

"Her necklace is gone," Ginger said as she shielded her eyes. "She was wearing the *Blue Desire*."

44

CHAPTER SIX

$\mathcal{T}$he next day, Ginger shared a late breakfast with Haley in the morning room. Ambrosia had dragged Felicia out of bed earlier—the latter quite literally kicking and screaming having got in late the night before. Ginger overheard them arguing in the passage.

Felicia: "I'm not feeling well! Besides, I should think I'm old enough to decide if I want to go to church or not."

Ambrosia: "You are never *old enough* to not attend church."

Felicia: "Ginger doesn't always go."

Ambrosia: "That is none of your concern."

Clement drove them to a parish nearby, bless his heart.

Mrs. Beasley, the cook, was doing her best to fatten Ginger and Haley up.

"I don't understand the way girls want to hide their figures nowadays with dresses that hang like sacks. Men like women with something to hold on to!" She adjusted her brassiere over her ample bosom as if to make the point.

Ginger bit her cheek to keep from chuckling at the doting older lady. Mrs. Beasley left the room humming the popular song, *Yes, we have no bananas . . .*

Ginger picked up on the catchy tune and sang, "We can positively affirm without fear of contradiction, That our raspberries are delicious; really delicious, Very delicious . . ."

Haley joined in and they belted out, *"But we have no bananas today!"*

Mrs. Beasley poked her head in, her round face red with embarrassment. She tried to hold in a smile then disappeared back into the kitchen. Ginger and Haley broke into a fit of giggles.

"I suppose that was rather unsophisticated of us," Ginger said, after a sip of tea.

"Rather." Haley said. She shook open the *Daily News,* sat it neatly on the table, then dunked a strip of toast into half of a soft-boiled egg. When Ginger had told her about the English tradition and called it Dippy Eggs with Soldiers, Haley had laughed.

Haley's American sensibilities probably wouldn't like her saying so, but Ginger thought she looked rather English at the moment.

"Apparently Vladimir Lenin is ill again," Haley said, her Bostonian accent erasing the illusion.

"You can't always trust the papers," Ginger said. Boss sat patiently on the floor by Ginger's feet, his little head tilted up and eyes beseeching. Ginger gave in and held out a piece of bacon which he gobbled gratefully. "Mr. Lenin isn't that old—only in his fifties."

"But why would they mislead with a story as big as this?"

"It's a British tradition. Tabloid news. Why we call these papers the 'rags.'"

"The New York papers are saying the same thing."

"Well, I hope it's not true. As bad as Lenin is, there's always worse waiting around the corner."

Haley hummed. "Stalin and Trotsky are already vying for the position."

"Then the news must be true," Ginger said. "The poor Russians. The war, the revolution, dictatorship. Their hardship continues on."

"At least the aristocrats had a means to escape," Haley said. Her voice sounded free of judgment, but Ginger knew her friend often struggled with the class system found in most European countries.

"Olga Pavlovna didn't get to enjoy her freedom for long," Ginger replied.

Haley held her coffee cup midair. "That is a tragedy." Eyeing Ginger over her mug, she added, "If you don't mind my saying so, you didn't seem too happy to see the chief inspector again. In fact you looked quite pale."

"Well, someone did just die in my shop."

"Of course." Haley had the good sense to change the subject. "Are you still searching for the missing boyfriend?"

"I beg you not to be crass, Haley. Mr. Green's not Felicia's gentleman friend, thank you very much."

Haley smirked over the rim of her coffee cup. "My apologies, *Lady Gold*."

Ginger pursed her lips in frustration. With whom or at what, she wasn't sure. That Haley was too American? Or that Ginger wasn't American enough?

"By the way," Haley said. "Who was that lady with Chief Inspector Reed?"

"What lady?" Ginger asked, feeling her heart ache again.

"The brunette who was clinging to him at the gala."

Ginger sipped her tea and set it down. She looked Haley in the eye.

"That was Emelia Reed, his wife."

Haley stared back at Ginger as if she'd just been slapped. "So he *does* have a wife."

Basil had failed to produce a wife for the last six months the two of them had known him, and Haley had often surmised that his ring was a ploy to keep away unwanted female attention. After all, he certainly was dashing.

"He definitely does."

Haley's shoulders sagged. "I'm so sorry."

"It's nothing."

Haley narrowed dark eyes. "It's not 'nothing.' It's rotten. And he's a louse."

"Why? He's done nothing wrong."

"He misled you. Trifled with your emotions."

Ginger inhaled, buoying her resolve. "I'm entirely responsible for my own emotions."

"Next time I see him, I'm going to let him have it."

"No, Haley, you're not. Basil has made his decision. It's good and right that he chose his wife."

Resigned, Haley sighed. "You're too good for him anyway." She straightened with a new idea. "What about that vicar? He seems nice."

"And I thought *I* was the matchmaker!" Ginger pushed away her empty plate, with its few remaining crumbs, and picked up her cup of tea. "Shall we move into the sitting room?"

Like the rest of the house, Ginger's sitting room had been redecorated over the winter. Instead of the Victorian style of dark, heavy colours with spaces overfull with furniture, paintings, and knickknacks, the colour palette was lighter—rose instead of wine, sage instead of jade, lemon instead of saffron—with new straight-lined furniture and *avant-garde* art hanging on the wall. *The Mermaid*, the only art piece unchanged, hung over the stone fireplace. A gift from her father to her mother, the mythical creature reminded Ginger of the first Mrs. Hartigan, with its bright eyes and long red hair. Boss added to the ambience as he snored blissfully on the dog bed in the corner beside the hearth.

"How are you spending the rest of your day?" Ginger asked after they were comfortably seated.

"I called Dr. Watts and he's agreed to let me help with the duchess' post-mortem."

"That's good of him."

Haley nodded. "I'll miss him when he's gone."

Ginger straightened. "He's going somewhere?"

"Dr. Watts is approaching retirement. Actually, he

brought in his replacement the other day, a new graduate."

"Have you met him?" Ginger asked.

"Yes."

"And?"

"It will be a big loss for the forensic community when Dr. Watts leaves."

"You don't like the new pathologist," Ginger said.

"I didn't say that." Rebellious dark curls escaped their faux bob and hung loosely around Haley's face. She pushed them behind her ears. "It's just—he's young."

"Younger than you?"

Haley scoffed. "He's my age. Only thirty-four."

"You're thirty-three."

"My birthday's coming up. That's not the point."

Ginger inclined her head. "What is the point?"

"Dr. Watts has years of experience."

"And now you'll be working under someone your own age."

Haley let out a short breath. "I'm being petty, I know."

"Maybe he'll surprise you."

"Maybe."

"What's the doctor's name?" Ginger asked.

"Manu Gupta"

Ginger's brow lifted. "From India? Interesting. How long before Dr. Watts retires?"

"Another year. Dr. Gupta is an intern at the moment."

"Nothing to worry about for a while, then."

A commotion could be heard in the entrance hall—someone with a female voice making a boisterous entrance—and in moments Felicia burst into the sitting room.

"I don't know why I let Grandmama drag me to church," she said sounding exasperated. "I really don't. She spends all her energy introducing me to bland and simple men of a certain social status. Really, I thought we were meant to go to church to meet *Jesus*."

"Your grandmother's intentions are good," Ginger said. "If somewhat misdirected."

Felicia sat on the settee beside Haley and pulled off her gloves. "I suppose. Now, have you any news?"

"News of what?" Haley asked.

In Felicia's flamboyant way, she relayed her angst over the disappearance of her acting colleague.

"Felicia, darling," Ginger said, "do you know if Angus had a disagreement with anyone? Did he owe money?"

Felicia's face crumpled, and she flopped into an empty chair. "Actually, I don't know Angus that well. We weren't at a place where he confided in me. Did you find any clues at his flat?"

"His toiletries are still there."

"Men don't worry about such things," Haley said. "They can always pick up a new toothbrush."

"He left his medicaments behind too."

The news produced a whimper from Felicia.

Haley frowned. "That is more worrying. Do you remember what they were?"

"Aspirin and ergotamine."

Haley hummed. "A sufferer of migraines."

Felicia's blue eyes flashed with hope. "Angus got bad

news and left straightaway to be with his family, forgetting his medicaments in the process."

"I asked Geordie about his family, love," Ginger said. "He's already called Angus's father. Angus hasn't been in touch."

Clive Pippins, or Pips as Ginger liked to call him, entered the sitting room. The loyal butler had served the Hartigan family for thirty years—Ginger's entire life.

"Telephone call for Miss Higgins," he announced.

Haley jumped. "That will be Dr. Watts."

Ginger called after her. "Keep me posted!"

"Will do."

Ginger had hoped for a telephone call herself. Surely, Basil would ring to let her know the latest developments on the murder case. Wouldn't he?

Perhaps those days were over.

"I'm going back to bed," Felicia said, following Haley out. "I'm simply exhausted."

Ginger spent the afternoon reading, or rather, struggling to read. It was terribly difficult to keep her mind focused on the words. She couldn't stop replaying the events of the gala, from Basil's unexpected attendance with his wife on his elbow to the murder of the beautiful duchess.

GINGER DIDN'T LIKE DRIVING in the dark, but when the sun set at 5 p.m. as it did in the month of January, there often weren't a lot of choices. The two-door Daimler was a decade old. Stored for almost as long, the automobile was in mint condition. The exterior was deep blue with a flat black carriage roof, and inside the seats were rich, brown leather. In contrast, the spokes of the tyres were a bright yellow, though darkened with mud from the winter rains.

Ginger set the ignition, the throttle and the choke before pushing the starter button with her grey Paul Poiret shoe. She clutched into reverse, exiting the garage without incident, and made her way east towards the City of London.

The streets of London were often chaotic with motorcars wrestling for room amongst horse-drawn carts and carriages, bicyclists, and pedestrians.

Driving past Geordie's flat, Ginger noted the light from the sitting room window shining into the night. With only a few gaslights in the area, the streets felt menacing in their gloom. Ginger was thankful Clement had recently replaced the Daimler's headlamps.

She approached St. George's in the City of London and brought the motorcar to a stop. Bright lights shone from the parish hall, and Ginger had to smile. Reverend Hill was there feeding the street children. The Child Wellness Project had recently been initiated by Ginger, and Oliver was keen to jump onboard. This was the first meal. Ginger entered the hall with enthusiasm.

Oliver Hill was billowy with wavy red hair just slightly brighter in tone than Ginger's. Though he sometimes had a nervous twitch around the eyes, they were gentle. His face was lined with kindness. They had bonded over their shared hair colour and laughed over the problems that only redheads would understand.

"It's hard to get lost in a crowd."

"I can't wear pink."

"Makes my face look pink!"

"Yes, especially when hot or embarrassed."

When Ginger had returned to London after visiting her husband's grave in Hertfordshire, she'd sought spiritual comfort and believed that providence had led her to St. George's Church and Reverend Hill. She'd stumbled upon St. George's after spotting young Scout in the area. He'd disappeared before she could call out to him and she'd almost driven off when something about the church garden and nearby graveyard called to her. Before she knew what she was doing, she was inside the church sitting on the back pew. After a few minutes, Reverend Hill had slipped in beside her and offered spiritual comfort.

Reverend Hill had helped her through many days of grief. Even though Daniel had been dead for over five years, Ginger hadn't found the strength to move on. She would never admit this aloud—though Haley knew—that Chief Inspector Basil Reed had something to do with her willingness to try.

"Lady Gold!" Reverend Hill said, smiling. "So good of you to come."

"I wouldn't miss the first meal sponsored by the Child Wellness Project for the world." Ginger took in the business of the hall. Tables had been set out and each one filled with eager children. "It looks like the meal programme is a big success."

"It doesn't take much to convince the children to come to church when food's involved." Oliver's eyes sparkled with satisfaction. It was clear he truly cared for each wayward soul.

The children ranged in age from seven to sixteen, including—Ginger was happy to note—her own young friends, the cousins Scout and Marvin Elliot.

She'd scoured the hall for Scout's poky blond hair and on finding him, smiled. Scout seemed to sense her because his pointy chin moved up and away from his plate of food. His gaze met hers. He broke into a crooked-toothed grin, his adult teeth making a big production of arriving and not in the least interested in behaving by showing up in a straight line.

"Missus!" he shouted over the din of the others focused on eating their mash.

"Scout!" Ginger said. She made long strides to the boy. Scout jumped off his bench and held out a small, grimy hand. Ginger didn't hesitate to place her white silk glove into it.

"Good to see ya, missus."

"And you, young Scout. I think you've grown since I last saw you."

"Really?"

"Really." It wasn't a lie. The lad was taller, if ever so slightly. He was destined to be small for his age. A lack of nutrition and a proper mother to feed one regularly could do that.

His older cousin, Marvin, who sat beside him greeted Ginger with the shyness of adolescence. "Madam," he said with a nod.

Ginger had met both boys on the SS *Rosa*, when she crossed from Boston to Liverpool. The boys had worked below deck and Scout had taken good care of Boss.

As if he could read her mind, Scout said, "'Ow's the old boy?"

"He's fine," Ginger said. "Getting lazy with the poor weather. I'm afraid he doesn't care for winter."

"Me neither, missus." Scout wiped a sleeve along the bottom of his nose.

Marvin cleared his throat and, glancing up at Ginger sheepishly, said, "I don't suppose ya 'ave a bit a work to toss our way, eh?"

The boys often helped Ginger. It was always mutually beneficial, not charity. "Actually, I do. I'm looking for someone." She displayed the photograph of Angus Green. Neither boy recognised him. And why would they? They weren't likely to go to the theatre.

"He lives in the area, just beyond St. Paul's. I would appreciate if you kept an eye out for him."

"And report back if we sees sumfin s'picious," Scout said with the confidence of someone who knew the streets.

"Exactly," Ginger said. She gave each boy three shillings. "If you see Mr. Green, or hear anyone talking about him, come back to St. George's and let Reverend Hill know. He'll ring me. Under no circumstances are you to approach him or anyone discussing him." Ginger wanted to make sure she never unintentionally put the boys in danger when she gave them these sorts of jobs. "Do you understand?"

"Yes, missus!" Scout beamed.

Marvin added. "We understand. We'll be careful."

"I do believe your dinner is getting cold." Ginger tousled up Scout's greasy hair. "Get back to your meal."

Ginger let Reverend Hill know when she was about to leave and he walked with her to the hall entrance.

"Reverend, you might not have heard, but an unfortunate incident happened in my shop last night."

Oliver Hill's ready smile disappeared. "Nothing too serious I hope?"

"Actually, it's quite serious. There's been a death."

"Oh, dear."

"I can't really say any more until the police release the details."

"I understand. I'll pray for you, Lady Gold."

"I appreciate that, Reverend. Thank you."

They were interrupted by Mrs. Davies, the church secretary. "Excuse me, Reverend. There's a phone call for Lady Gold."

Ginger expressed her surprise. "For me?"

"Yes, madam."

"Who is it?"

"He says he's a chief inspector from Scotland Yard. Sorry, madam, I didn't catch his name."

Basil must've called Hartigan House and learned of Ginger's whereabouts. What would prevail upon him to ring for her here?

"I'll say my goodbyes now, Lady Gold," Reverend Hill said. "I must get back to the children. Mrs. Davies will accompany you to the kitchen."

"Very well, Reverend Hill," Ginger said pleasantly. "Goodbye for now."

Once in the kitchen, Ginger picked up the receiver."

"Lady Gold? It's Chief Inspector Reed."

"Hello, Chief Inspector." Ginger noted with a prick in

her heart how they had reverted back to addressing each other formally. An invisible barrier stood between them now that Emelia Reed was in the picture. "What can I do for you?"

"Would you like to join me in my interviews tomorrow? You have a special insight—it was your store. Plus, it's often helpful when interviewing women to have another in the room."

Ginger admitted that she and Basil made a good investigative team, but her heart was divided. The best medicine for her emotional angst was to stay away from the man who caused it. Yet, Feathers & Flair's reputation was on the line, not to mention her own. The best thing for her business and her social wellbeing would be to solve this case quickly.

"I would like that," she said.

Though Ginger, technically, was a suspect, Basil didn't seem to mind.

"Brilliant," he said. "I'll pick you up in the morning."

Ginger recalled Haley's aggression aimed at Basil due to what she perceived as a great offence against Ginger, and didn't want to risk a confrontation. "Is it okay if I meet you at the Yard?"

CHAPTER SEVEN

*W*hen Ginger pulled into the parking area behind New Scotland Yard, Basil was already waiting in his forest-green Austin 7. On seeing her, he exited his motorcar and opened the passenger door. Ginger inhaled to fortify herself. So what that Basil Reed was dapper, intelligent and a gentleman? So deuced what!

She would be professional. Her personal feelings were of no consequence when a lady lay dead in the mortuary and a murderer was on the loose.

"Good morning," Basil said.

"Good morning, Chief Inspector."

Ginger slid onto her seat, her silk stockings appearing briefly from underneath her coat. Basil was good enough to pretend not to notice. He closed the door softly and hopped in, quickly starting the motorcar and turning up the heat.

"Where to?" Ginger asked.

"Lady Isla Lyon and the Princess Sophia von Altenhofen."

Ginger understood why the former German princess was on the list—her dislike of the grand duchess had been apparent, but why Lady Lyon?

Basil anticipated her question. "Lady Lyon is known to the police."

Ginger didn't bother to keep her shock from showing. "Whatever for?"

"I'm afraid she has a propensity to take things that don't belong to her."

"She's a thief?"

"Lord Lyon has been covering for her for years. He's always returned the items and paid recompense to the rightful owners."

"Oh, dear."

Lord and Lady Lyon lived in a prestigious town house in Westminster overlooking the Thames. When Basil knocked on the door, a short, plump butler answered. Basil made introductions.

"I'm Chief Inspector Basil Reed and this is Lady Gold. We would like to see Lady Lyon. She's expecting us."

"This way, sir, madam."

Lord and Lady Lyon were in the drawing room. Lady Isla Lyon, a good quarter-century younger than her husband, was attractive with bright eyes and a salon-crafted bob. She lounged on a luxurious settee, reading as if she didn't have a care in the world. Lord Lyon sat bent over at a monstrous dark-walnut desk, an ink-filled quill between his fingers. An older gent who hadn't yet adapted to the fountain pen, it seemed.

The butler announced the visitors and both Lord and Lady Lyon stood.

"Very good of you to come," Lord Lyon said as if he had been the one to instigate the meeting. He was a large man, both in height and girth, and shook hands with the confidence of a man used to getting his way. Lady Lyon smiled and offered tea. Her demeanour was much like her husband's—as if Ginger and Basil's visit was a social call and nothing more.

Ginger caught Basil's look—distinctly unamused.

Sitting, Basil said, "I hope you haven't misinterpreted the nature of our visit."

"I'm assuming it has to do with the sad news we heard about the grand duchess," Lord Lyon said. He removed a pipe from its tray and lit it. "So sad, especially for one so beautiful."

Ginger bit her tongue. The grand duchess' demise was tragic but not any more so than a poor fellow suffering a similar tragedy.

"That is the reason," Basil admitted. He sipped his tea, placed it back on the saucer, and returned it to the coffee table in front of him. His gaze moved from the lord to the lady. "My enquiries may prove distasteful, but I'll be as delicate as possible."

"Proceed," Lord Lyon said as if Basil needed his permission.

"I'm afraid an item of jewellery has gone missing."

Lady Lyon's slender fingers went to her naked throat, and on failing to find anything there, returned to her lap.

"What are you saying?" Lord Lyon's gruff tone was hard to miss.

"The grand duchess' necklace," Ginger said gently, "the *Blue Desire*, is missing." She explained further. "It's an infamous blue diamond teardrop on a silver chain."

"Infamous, you say," Lord Lyon muttered. "Probably taken by whoever killed her,"

Basil stared straight at him.

The chief inspector's meaning dawned on the older man. "Surely, you're not insinuating—"

"Lord Lyon," Basil said. "I'm simply looking for answers. It's possible that the grand duchess may have lost her necklace before her demise."

"You think I might have taken it," Lady Lyon said weakly. She looked to Ginger. "It's a nasty habit I have. A strong urge just comes over me and I can't help myself." She turned to Basil. "But I promise you, I didn't take the *Blue Desire*."

Ginger noticed how Lady Lyon hadn't promised she hadn't taken anything, and made a mental note to have Madame Roux check the supplies.

"What time did you and Lady Lyon leave the gala?" Basil asked.

Lord Lyon shrugged. "Just after eleven, I suppose. The same as most of Lady Gold's guests."

Basil scribbled in his notepad—Ginger couldn't imagine what—but perhaps he was only making a show. To keep the lord and lady on their toes.

Basil finished his tea and stood. "We shan't bother you any further. Thank you for your time."

Lord Lyon summoned his butler who showed them out.

"I don't think it's them," Ginger said.

"Is that your intuition speaking again?"

Ginger didn't bother answering. Once they were in the car she asked, "Have you checked their finances?"

"Lord Lyon is as rich as he claims. Not only does he own his London townhouse, he also has a large country estate and owns several businesses."

"So money isn't a motive."

Basil conceded. "No."

"Lady Lyon has a sickness, like gambling. Sneaky thievery. I don't think she has it in her to actually hurt someone."

"That doesn't mean she didn't take the diamond."

Basil directed his motorcar through the west end of St. James's Park and into Piccadilly. "Princess Sophia von Altenhofen has taken a room at the Ritz."

"Oh, I love the Ritz!"

The five-storey sandstone hotel had Grecian-style arches along the pedestrian pavement. Each room had tall windows with wrought iron Juliet balconies.

Basil handed his keys over to a parking valet and they were ushered up the steps to the main revolving door. The doorman, dressed in a long black suit jacket, shiny black shoes and a top hat, ushered them inside.

The entrance hall was circular with a high-domed ceiling, a massive glass chandelier, and oriental carpeting. Blood-red carpeting covered the steps that curled up to the next floor.

Basil approached the front desk—curved to fit the room, well-lit with electric lamps—and asked the clerk to ring for Princess von Altenhofen.

"Tell her we'll be waiting in the lounge."

"Are you ordering something," Ginger said when they'd chosen seats.

"A club soda. I don't drink alcohol when I'm on duty," Basil said.

Ginger ordered a white coffee.

The German princess who had lost her nobility, arrived with the panache of a Hollywood star. Her blond hair was perfectly coiffed, framing a square chin. Her eyes, though not heavily made up, were striking nevertheless under sharply manicured brows. Two rounds of rouge highlighted her cheeks. She threw a feather boa around her neck as she strolled over, head held high, her former royal status apparent in her posture and gait. It was no longer proper to bow before the German lady, and Ginger stifled the inclination to do so.

"Hello, Chief Inspector, Lady Gold," she said claiming the lone empty seat at the round table. "To what do I owe the pleasure?"

"Princess Sophia," Basil said. "Thank you for agreeing to see us."

Ginger knew that the princess didn't have a choice. The princess probably knew that as well, but everyone operated under the polite façade.

A waiter approached with a drink the princess had yet to order; evidently the house knew her preference and that she was always thirsty. She removed a rolled cigarette from her gold cigarette box and placed it in an ivory holder. She smiled at Basil who in turn produced a lighter.

"*Danke.*"

Basil leaned back and crossed his legs. To Ginger's

surprise he joined the princess, producing a cigarette of his own. She knew he was a smoker, most men—and many women, if the truth were told—were, she'd just never seen him light up during an investigation before.

Had the habit become more frequent since reuniting with his wife? Ginger chose not to dwell on what that could mean, if anything.

"Princess Sophia," Ginger began, "you must have heard by now that the grand duchess Olga Pavlovna Orlova has perished."

"It was in the papers."

"Did you know the grand duchess?" Basil asked.

"No."

"But I saw you talking to her at the gala last night," Ginger said. "You appeared angry."

Princess Sophia blew a long stream of smoke out of the side of her mouth, and picked up her glass.

"You are mistaken."

"I saw it."

"Fine. She interrupted my discussion with Monsieur Molyneux. Very rude of her. That was the emotion you saw, Lady Gold. Frustration."

"Not contempt?"

The princess shifted a shoulder and inhaled from the ivory tip of her cigarette holder.

"I heard you tell Lady Meredith that the grand duchess was not what she seemed," Ginger said. "What did you mean by that?"

"Nobody is what they seem. Am I right? You, for instance, are English, yet there is something quite . . . let me see . . . American about you." She turned her attention to Basil and smirked. "You wear a wedding ring, yet your eyes linger—"

Basil sat upright. "Have you had the opportunity to meet the grand duchess before last night? Perhaps in Germany or Russia?"

"I can tell you most honestly, I had not met the grand duchess before last night."

"Do you collect valuable jewellery?" Basil asked.

"When I can. It's been difficult since the war."

"What did you think of the *Blue Desire* necklace the grand duchess was wearing?" Ginger asked.

The princess' eyes twinkled with amusement. "Why?"

Basil answered, "It's been taken."

Princess Sophia laughed. "Well, I almost feel sorry for the thief."

"Why do you say that?" Ginger asked.

The princess' mirth remained. "Because that *Blue Desire* was a fake."

CHAPTER EIGHT

"It's not uncommon for the rich to own fakes, or pastes as they are often referred to, replicas of their authentic pieces," Ginger explained as Basil drove. "The fear of theft . . ."

Basil nodded. "Heavy, transparent flint glass known as strass stones."

"Yes. They refract light very much like the genuine article. The blue diamond the grand duchess wore was quite convincing."

Basil changed gears and came to a stop to allow a group of pedestrians to pass by. They were in Whitechapel heading for the London Royal Free Hospital. Haley had been called in to prepare for the grand duchess' post-mortem yesterday with the surgery scheduled for this morning. Ginger was looking forward to hearing the results.

"Princess von Altenhofen knows something, and she's not telling," Ginger said.

"The question is," Basil added, "is it something we care

to know or is she trifling with us. We need more information on all the foreign royals. What can you tell me about the Romanian countess, Andreea Balcescu?"

"Not much, I'm afraid. She came in once the day before the gala. I hadn't met her or even heard of her before then."

"I'm afraid you're not alone. My inquiries about foreign nobles visiting England have failed to produce a Romanian countess of any kind."

"Are you saying she's arrived by illegal means?"

"It's quite likely."

"She might be our killer, then."

"Or merely our thief. It could've been a crime of opportunity. The 'countess' may have discovered the body, and instead of reporting the crime, stole the blue diamond."

"But the necklace is a fake."

"Which means we're looking for a disappointed imposter."

As if the countess might suddenly materialise, Ginger scanned the pavement as they drove. "Where exactly have you looked?"

"There are only a few select hotels that the royals frequent."

"The Ritz, the Savoy, and Brown's Hotel."

Basil agreed. "Those are the top three."

London traffic was in a snarl and it took longer than usual to find a spot to park near the hospital. They went directly to the lower level where the mortuary was located and asked for Dr. Watts.

"Come in." Dr. Watts was a beefy-looking middle-aged

man with thick white hair, and a gentle face. "We're ready for you."

"We?" Ginger prompted. Her eyes searched for the curly hair of her friend. Instead of Haley, a man dressed in a physician's white coat turned around. Before her stood a striking figure, exotic with caramel skin, black glossy hair neatly trimmed, and eyes like polished brass.

"Allow me to introduce you to my new colleague, Dr. Manu Gupta."

Ginger swallowed. *Oh, mercy.* Poor, poor Haley. No wonder she'd looked like a wilted wallflower when speaking of him. No lady likes to come second in beauty to a *man.* Even Ginger, who considered herself relatively attractive, found Dr. Gupta's presence intimidating.

He shook hands with Basil and Ginger, welcoming them.

Basil cleared his throat.

"Do you have a report prepared, Dr. Watts?"

"I do."

Dr. Gupta showed his efficiency by having the requested document at the ready. He handed it to Basil.

"It's a cervical fracture." Dr. Gupta said as he stared at them. "Her neck was broken, between the first and second vertebrae. Bruising along the neck indicated the strength of the killer was in the left hand."

"The killer is left-handed?" Basil said.

Dr. Watts nodded. "Though left-handed people are often ambidextrous, right-handed people are mainly dependent on their right side for anything that requires strength or dexterity. Snapping a neck in this fashion requires both, and evidence points to a left-handed perpetrator."

"Are you saying this crime was committed by a man?" Ginger said. "There were very few present."

"I would interview them all if I were you," Dr. Watt's said.

"It's possible an attack like this could've been committed by a well-trained lady," Dr. Gupta added.

Ginger recalled the self-defence training she had done during the war as a member of the secret service. She'd seen firsthand how a confident lady could break a neck as easily as any man.

"Besides the neck damage, was there anything else of note?" Basil asked.

"There was skin under the victim's fingernails," Dr. Gupta said. "Whoever did this will have scratches on his or her hands or forearms. At least until they heal."

With those words, the race to find the killer began. Basil and Ginger shared a glance. They had to get on with it.

"Please let me know if anything new comes to light," Basil said. He doffed his hat. "Good day, gentlemen."

Back in the Austin, Basil gripped the steering wheel and whistled. "A left-handed killer with scratch marks on his or her hands or forearms."

"Miss von Altenhofen wore gloves the whole time we spoke to her," Ginger said. "I don't know if she's our killer, but she's guilty of something."

"Lady Lyon removed her gloves when she poured the tea," Basil said. "Did you notice any scratches?"

Ginger shook her head. "No. However, Lord Lyon kept

his leather gloves on the whole time. Do you find that rather odd?"

"Gloves are part of the outfit. Lord Lyon is an elegant dresser."

"You removed your gloves," Ginger said.

"That is true."

Basil drove them back to Scotland Yard.

"What are you going to do now?" Ginger asked.

"I'm going to make a few calls to the foreign embassies." He checked his wristwatch. "I'm awaiting word on what to do with the grand duchess' body. She fled Russia, so I assume the embassy will take responsibility for it."

Ginger stepped out of the motorcar in tandem with Basil. They stared at each other over the roof. Ginger forced an air of professionalism, staying emotionally distant. "Please ring me if you discover anything new, Chief Inspector."

"I shall." The tenderness in his gaze made her stomach flip-flop. "Thank you for joining me today, Lady Gold."

Ginger was determined not to look over her shoulder at Basil as she walked away. Let him think she didn't care —that he hadn't deeply hurt her.

CHAPTER NINE

*M*rs. Schofield had become a regular visitor of Ambrosia's, much to the dowager Lady Gold's barely concealed dislike.

The door to the drawing room was open when Ginger returned, and she could hear the conversation bellowing along the high ceilings into the entrance hall.

"Did you know that the daughter of the Earl of Dunsworth is competing in the winter games in February —what do they call it now? Yes, the Olympics! In France."

"Langley told me about it," Ambrosia said. "Skating figures or some such thing. Quite unbecoming behaviour for a young lady of her status."

"Why shouldn't women enjoy sports like the men do?" Mrs. Schofield countered. "Men have so many advantages and privileges as it is."

"I miss the old way. So much simpler when everyone knew their place. My Felicia—I just don't understand the child. I feel like I need to put lead in her shoes, just to keep her from floating away."

Poor Ambrosia. The war had brought many changes to English society, and Ginger's dear grandmother-in-law was finding it hard to adjust. Though a grandmother herself, Mrs. Schofield seemed younger at heart.

"Germany, of course, is not invited," Mrs. Schofield said.

"I should hope not!"

Ginger thought it a good time to poke her head in and say hello. The drawing room had been the first room at Hartigan House to have undergone a décor transformation. Gone were the long, heavy dark curtains, and the excessive wall decorations. In their place were light sheers, geometric wallpaper, and paintings of her parents when they had been about the same age as Ginger was now. A grand piano sat in the corner, woefully underplayed. The room was pleasant and she was happy Ambrosia had decided to make use of it. Perhaps, once this case was solved, Ginger would throw a party.

"So good to see you again, Lady Gold," Mrs. Schofield said. "Alfred is coming for dinner tonight. If you're free, you could join us."

Ginger smiled at the older lady. She was always trying to set Ginger up with her grandson.

"I'm afraid I've already made plans for this evening, but thank you so much for your kind offer. Do say hello to Alfred."

Alfred Schofield had made quite an impression on Ginger when he had attended her last soirée, and not a good one. He'd flirted shamelessly with her, and Felicia as well, all whilst being involved with someone else. Ginger had no intention of dining with Alfred, now or ever.

Ginger circled up the staircase, removing her leather gloves as she went. Once in the bedroom that had been hers as a child, she slipped out her hatpin, removed her hat—a black felt wide-brim adorned with a broad red feather—and dropped it into its hatbox. She ran fingers through her hair, lifting the bob where the hat had pressed it down.

The pink and blue colours of her childhood room had been redecorated with gold and ivory furnishings. A bed with an extravagantly carved wooden headboard and footboard was set against one wall. Two striped ivory and gold chairs sat in front of the long windows, perfect for catching the daylight over tea and for journal writing. A full-length ornately trimmed mirror stood in the corner near a matching dressing table, and beside it was an old gramophone.

Boss lay at the foot of her bed and watched her with interest. Ginger smiled and went to him, scrubbing his head. "If I'm the most intriguing thing you've seen today, then your life is truly boring. I must change that." She lifted him like a baby and cuddled him in her arms. "I think I shall take you with me more often." The dog loved her unconditionally and she appreciated the support. Especially now when her heart was heavy. Every time she thought of Basil, she would replace his image in her mind with Boss'. She had a feeling she'd be thinking about Boss a lot in the next few days.

Ginger kissed the pup's head and placed him back on the bed before turning to her wardrobe. She changed into a simple tea dress of soft silk and donned a pair of green satin slippers. She called for Boss and he followed her. They met Ambrosia and Langley on the landing.

"How was your visit with Mrs. Schofield?" Ginger asked.

"Exhausting. I don't know where that lady gets her energy. By the way, have you seen Felicia? I can't keep track of the child."

"I believe she's at the theatre, rehearsing for a new audition."

"Oh, dear Lord." Ambrosia sighed with defeat. "Langley, bring me a pot of tea."

The willowy maid bobbed and headed back down the stairs. Ginger and Boss followed her as far as the sitting room where Ginger helped herself to a glass of wine—a 1921 French merlot—and relaxed in front of the fire. Someone had recently been in to feed and stoke it as the flames burned brightly. Ginger curled up in its warmth.

The front door opened, and Ginger heard the shuffle of someone, she assumed Haley, removing her outer winter wear. Moments later her assumption was confirmed. Haley entered and smiled at Ginger.

"Now, that's more like it."

"Please join me."

Haley moved to the sideboard, poured herself a drink, and lounged on the settee. Like Ginger, she removed her hat and pulled out the hairpins that created her faux bob. A long dark, wavy ponytail landed on one shoulder. To settle herself on the settee, she tugged on the skirt of her wool suit. More than once Ginger had tried to talk Haley into allowing her seamstress to raise her hems, but Haley would have none of it. "Medicine and vanity don't mix," she'd said.

"We missed you at the hospital mortuary today," Ginger said.

"I had a class I didn't want to miss. Ballistics as it ties to forensic science. It's a relatively new field of study." Haley grinned. "I mastered the class, having been one of the few to have actually fired a weapon and picked up discharged bullets and casings, thanks to the second amendment."

"Sounds exciting."

"Every bullet can be traced back to the firearm it was discharged from. The discharge leaves a distinct marking."

"Interesting," Ginger said with all sincerity. "I'd love to see examples."

"Sure. Just visit me at the medical school someday."

"I will."

Haley scanned the room as if looking for something. "Where's the boss?" Haley liked to refer to Boss as "the boss," as if the dog ran the whole show. Boss liked to think he did.

"I thought he was on his bed. He must've gone in search of food." Ginger stared at Haley. "Do you miss Boston?"

"Your dog or the city?"

Ginger laughed. "The city."

"Sometimes. I miss baseball and peanut butter."

"Really?" Ginger said. "I didn't take you as a sports fan."

"I'm not just talking about watching the game. I love to play it."

Ginger leaned in. "I didn't know that about you." She smiled. "I have no problem believing you were a tomboy, though."

"I still am and proud of it. Being the only girl among three brothers helps."

"Indeed."

"Enough about me. How was your day?"

Ginger relayed the interviews with Lord and Lady Lyon and Princess Sophia.

"I'm not sure which is more alarming," Haley said. "That Lady Lyon is a kleptomaniac or that the blue diamond the grand duchess was wearing was a fake."

"Both are alarming."

Haley raised a brow. "And Basil?"

"What of him?" Ginger said. She wouldn't admit that even the mention of his name was a stab in the heart.

"Is it not strange to go on these interviews with him as if nothing had happened between you?"

"Nothing *has* happened. And yes it's strange, but we're both professionals."

"Of course."

Ginger was ready to turn the tables. She stared at Haley over her glass. "I met Dr. Gupta today."

Haley's eyes darted to Ginger and back to her drink. "And?"

"He's nice."

"Very nice," Haley conceded.

"And very intelligent."

"You can't fool him."

"You forgot to mention that he was a Greek, or rather, an Indian god."

"Holy mackerel, Ginger!" Haley threw her head back. "You can't imagine how hard it is to work with him. My physiology betrays me. Dry mouth, rapid heartbeat, and an annoying flush to my cheeks. I find it very difficult to focus when he's in the room."

"Oh, mercy, Haley."

"I'm being idiotic, that's what. I'm like a broom leaning up against the statue of David."

"Oh, come on. You're too hard on yourself. Yes, your wardrobe could use a sprucing up, but you're frightfully attractive."

Haley scoffed. "Don't patronise me."

"Haley, I'm not. So, maybe you're not conventionally beautiful, but you have very pleasant features, and I'm not patronising you when I say that. It's true. Your eyes are lovely, you have gorgeous dark lashes, and you have an appealing mouth."

Haley laughed heartily. "Oh Ginger, I love you! And I apologise for being vain. I intend to stop it right now. I'm training to be a doctor. The last thing I need is to get caught up in a romance. Besides with a face like that, I'm sure Dr. Gupta must already have someone."

Ginger thought it quite likely. The Indian population in London had grown significantly since the empire had acquired India a century ago. Dr. Gupta probably was already attached to a pretty Indian girl. A match with someone as white as Haley would be difficult, even in a progressive cosmopolitan city such as London.

CHAPTER TEN

*H*aving made no headway on the murder case, Ginger decided it was a good time to visit Angus Green's parents.

It took forty minutes to drive to Battersea over the Albert Bridge, and Ginger had to stop to ask directions for the address she'd got from Peter McGuire, the stage manager.

The large two-storey brick house was set back from the road and had a long drive lined with hedges. It was clear that the Green family had money.

Ginger tapped on the thick wooden door, using the brass knocker shaped like a lion with a ring in its mouth. How would she approach this? She certainly didn't want to cause Mr. and Mrs. Green undue worry.

A gentleman opened the door. He stood with his back straight, hands on hips, and an air of self-importance. Ginger saw a resemblance to Angus Green in his eyes.

"Mr. Green?"

"Yes. Who are you?"

"My name is Ginger Gold. My sister-in-law is a friend of your son's."

"Which one?"

"Angus."

Mr. Green snorted. "What kind of trouble is the young fool in now?"

"Do you have a moment? May I come in?"

Mr. Green stepped clear and waved Ginger inside.

The sitting room was tidy and clean, but Ginger got the feeling the room wasn't used much.

"Is Mrs. Green at home?"

"My wife passed away eight years ago."

"I'm sorry."

Mr. Green shrugged. "I'd offer you tea, but . . ."

"No, it's quite all right. I won't be long."

"Very well. What's Angus gone and done now?"

"I don't know if he's done anything, actually. It's just, Felicia, my sister-in-law, is worried because he failed to show up for the final two nights of the play they were in together."

Mr. Green chortled. "A play? Aren't all the men who do that . . ." He stopped short as if remembering there was a lady in the room. "I knew I should've held his trust fund until he was thirty-five."

Mr. Green showed no concern for his son's safety.

"Is this kind of behaviour normal for Angus?"

"What's normal for Angus? Nothing's normal, that's what! He could've gone to university, could've been a doctor, could've married a baroness. At least his brother, Andrew, has some sense."

"When was the last time you heard from Angus?"

"Christmas. What a circus that was. Ever since Maggie died, it's just been the three of us bachelors. It's only me here now. I have a woman come in to clean and cook for me."

Ginger heard the loneliness that he tried desperately to hide among his words.

"I'm sure Angus is fine. My intention isn't to cause alarm. I'll let my sister-in-law know that Angus, the free spirit he appears to be, has simply gone on his way."

"I'm sorry he's been an imbecile. He's always off on one lark or the other. I'm sure your sister—Felicia is it?— didn't deserve an idiot like him."

"Oh, they weren't together. Just friends."

Mr. Green blinked slowly like he'd caught her in a lie. Angus Green was dashing and charming. Ginger doubted, as Mr. Green apparently did, that the young Green had women who were merely friends.

"I'll bother you no longer."

For the first time, Mr. Green smiled. "Actually, I've enjoyed the deviation, Miss—"

"Mrs. Gold."

There was a flicker of disappointment in Mr. Green's eyes, and Ginger said nothing to correct the man's mistaken assumption she was married.

GINGER RETURNED to Regent Street and parked her motorcar.

"Lady Gold!" The raspy voice belonged to Blake Brown. He huffed as he caught up to her.

"Hello, Mr. Brown," Ginger said. "Out for a run?"

"No," he said with a heave. He held up a hand. "Allow me a moment to get my breath."

Ginger had pity on him and stopped.

"I know why you've risked your vascular health to catch up with me. It's regarding the death of Olga Pavlovna in my shop."

"Yes! Why did you not call me back for the story? I thought we had an . . . understanding."

"I'm not sure what understanding that might be Mr. Brown. The police have taken over the investigation. I'm assuming that's how you found out?"

"Well, yes," Mr. Brown admitted. "I do have a contact at the Yard."

"Then what do you need from me?"

"An exclusive. Your shop, and I might add, your reputation are on the line. Don't you want to give your side?"

"My side? I'm hardly responsible for the violent actions of others, and am actually a victim since, as you've said, the news has tainted my business."

Blake Brown started writing fiercely with his small chewed-up pencil on a well-worn notepad. "Can I quote you on that?"

"No! Please, Mr. Brown. You can't print anything I say right now!"

"Can't I at least ask you questions? How long was the grand duchess dead before she was discovered?"

"No comment."

"I understand there was a jewel theft involved. What do you know about the blue diamond the grand duchess wore that night?"

"No comment."

"Are you under investigation?"

"What? No! I had nothing to do with the grand duchess' death. And no comment."

"Actually, that was a comment. Don't you find it odd that death seems to follow you?"

Ginger frowned at how Blake Brown's comment had become truth since she'd left Boston for England.

"I find it incredibly annoying that *you're* following me, Mr. Brown. And if you don't desist, I'll have to file a complaint."

"Very well. I think I have what I need." Blake Brown smiled and tipped his hat.

Ginger stopped dead in her tracks and scowled at the back of the man as he sauntered away with the contentment of a cat who'd just eaten a bird.

Though opening hours had begun, Feathers & Flair was still closed to the public. Ginger tapped on the glass of the front door, and a nervous Dorothy West let her inside.

"Oh, madam, it's dreadful. I can't stop seeing that poor lady on the floor of the dressing room, all blue in the face. I don't know how you manage to go on."

"We all must manage, Dorothy." Ginger considered the shop assistant and not for the first time, second-guessed her decision to employ her. "You must pull yourself together. I intend to have the doors open within an hour, and you must be ready."

"Yes, madam."

On hearing Ginger's voice, Madame Roux looked up from the cash register, a bundle of receipts in her hands. "I haven't had a chance to settle these, but from a cursory glance I can say the gala did quite well, financially speaking."

Socially speaking, it could be a lame duck. Ginger glanced at the door, and not one customer was outside hoping to get in.

"I brought in extra cleaning women because of the gala," Madame Roux said. "They should be finished shortly."

Ginger was pleased with how spotless the front show-room looked. Emma Miller was busy tidying up the window display. All evidence of the gala and the crime had been removed from Feathers & Flair. The floors shone with polish, the electric lights highlighted all the latest fashions on racks and mannequins. Not a spot of dust could be found anywhere. Even the gold mouldings on the ceilings had been wiped down.

"Oh, Madame Roux, before I forget, please see that all sales are accounted for."

Madame Roux stared back. "Are you suggesting that someone took something without paying?"

"Not at all." Her mind went to Lady Lyon's confession. "Well, maybe. I've come across a distressing piece of information, and I just want to make sure."

"Very well."

Ginger assisted Emma in restocking the gowns and accessories on the ground floor. Empty shelves, hooks, and gaps in the displays would never do. If it hadn't been for the murder, they would've been ready on time.

"Has anyone been upstairs?" Ginger asked. "Dorothy?"

"Yes. Rack dresses weren't of interest to last night's

crowd. Everything is in order. I've tidied up, just the same."

Ginger unlocked the doors at ten o'clock and felt a wave of relief when an actual line assembled. The faces were younger, and quite likely the second level crowd.

"Welcome to Feathers & Flair, ladies."

"Is it true someone died here last night?"

"I heard it was a royal from the Middle East."

"Russia, Maggie," one of the girls corrected.

"Well, that's east, isn't it?"

Ginger frowned. She wanted real customers, not tabloid chasers.

"New dresses have come in from New York. Miss West would be happy to take you upstairs to view them."

"Is that where the lady died?"

"It's true that we had an unfortunate incident in the shop last night, and the police are investigating. I can't tell you more than what you've already read in the papers. Now, if you're interested in seeing the new line . . ."

"Oh, I'm dying to see it."

"Marjorie!"

"Oops, I didn't mean to use the word, *dying*. That's not bad luck, is it? I'm not going to die here too, am I?"

"I can assure you," Ginger said, holding her patience with these silly girls on a thread. "No one is going to die here today."

Ginger froze. She'd said those same words to Blake Brown last night.

Unlike the younger crowd, "polite society" was too well-bred to venture into a shop where a murder of one of their own had occurred. Ginger tried not to fret over the lack of shop visitors and kept herself busy in the back with Emma. She was sewing an evening gown for Lady Fitzhugh, her nose low, intent on doing good work.

"It's so much easier to make a gown now than it was before the war," Emma said. "The amount of fabric needed for today's fashions is almost a third less. Down seven yards - from nineteen to twelve!"

"This is why the average lady can now afford to wear the trends," Ginger said.

"It's fabulous!"

"I agree."

Ginger mused over Emma's drawings on the large sketchpad on the table. Emma really was very good.

Not wanting the young designer to feel like she was being watched, Ginger took a look upstairs for herself.

No wonder the upper level of Feathers & Flair had grown popular: Chiffon frocks with charming simplicity in orchid, rose, or white, and each with a large flower on the hip; Georgette crepe dresses with an attached cape that formed the sleeves, and hip band rosette ornaments, in green, navy blue or grey; Evening gowns of chiffon with flange drapery from the left shoulder, generously embroidered front and back with crystal and rhinestone, in orchid or grey.

Ginger noted one section that hung unevenly. The gaggle of girls from earlier that morning had likely rifled through. She took a moment to straighten a shawl on its hanger. A particular one caught her eye—winter-white tulle with an Egyptian print. Ginger recognised it right away. *How had Olga Pavlovna's shawl got here?*

Ginger held the shawl up to the light and noticed a

darker patch along one seam. Close inspection revealed a slender pocket had been sewn to the thicker edging. Poking with a fingernail, she pulled out a flattened roll of cigarette paper. Ginger opened the paper and found writing, but it appeared to be gibberish—W533o 8h 849h 975 wt90 @$. She blinked as understanding dawned. The scribbling wasn't gibberish. It was *code.*

"Lady Gold?"

Ginger turned at Dorothy's voice. She'd been so consumed with her discovery she hadn't heard the girl come up.

"Yes?"

"Telephone for you."

Ginger quickly slipped the paper into her dress pocket and headed down the steps with the shawl over her arm to the cash desk where she picked up the telephone receiver.

Ginger's pulse jumped at the sound of Basil Reed's voice.

"What can I do for you, Chief Inspector?"

"I need to interviewLord and Lady Whitmore. Would you like to accompany me?"

Think Boss, Boss, Boss.

"Certainly. I'd be happy to."

"Terrific. I'll pick you up in half an hour."

"And Chief Inspector, I have something I'm sure you'll want to see."

CHAPTER ELEVEN

Ginger climbed into Basil's Austin and immediately presented the cigarette paper.

Basil handled it carefully and frowned.

"I found it in a shawl pocket upstairs in my shop," Ginger said.

"Whose shawl?"

"It belonged to the grand duchess."

Basil shot her a look. "Is that so?"

"Yes. But that doesn't mean she was the one to take it upstairs. A shawl is easy enough to conceal. Folded it could fit into a handbag or even the pocket of a suit jacket."

Basil's forehead buckled. "These numbers and letters, what do they mean?"

"I don't know. It's code."

Basil stared at her. "Code? As in espionage?"

"Perhaps."

"Why was it in your shop?"

"Someone placed it there intending that another would retrieve it later."

"Except someone killed the grand duchess before she could find it."

"Unless she was the one who placed it there for another."

"But why would someone kill her, if they were working together?"

Ginger pursed her lips. "There must be a third person trying to prevent the communication."

"I'll have to hand it in to the Yard," Basil said as he started up the motorcar. "And hope that someone can make sense of it."

"Of course." Ginger had expected to hand it over, which was why she'd made a copy, now tucked away in her handbag.

"Why are you interviewing the Whitmores?" Ginger asked once they were on their way. Did Basil know about Lord Whitmore's involvement in the secret service?

"Lady Whitmore rang the Yard asking to speak to us."

"*She* instigated the interview?"

Basil nodded. "Do you have any idea why?"

"Only that she's the most notorious gossip in high society—a regular contributor to the papers, or rather, a regular 'anonymous' source."

"Hungry for attention, then?" Basil said.

"You could say that."

"Enough that she'd kill for it?"

Ginger jerked her head to stare back at Basil. "Dear Lord, you're serious."

"Dead serious. Forgive the pun. I've seen much weaker

motives in my line of work. Would you say that Lady Whitmore was, uh, unhinged?"

"Do you think that's what brought on her ailment? It was a ruse to keep the attention away from the body in the next room?"

"And gives her an alibi of sorts."

Lord and Lady Whitmore lived in a house as grand as Hartigan House and in the same Kensington area as well, on the other side of Mrs. Schofield's property.

Basil pointed to the well-kept three-storey limestone house. "Is that it?"

"Yes."

Basil parked at the kerb. Ginger glanced at Hartigan House, but there was no movement. Mallowan Court was quiet with the rain keeping the wise indoors.

Basil pushed the doorbell. The three-chime bell announcing their presence could be heard through the ornate wooden door. A butler answered.

"I'm Chief Inspector Basil Reed, and this is Lady Gold. I believe Lady Whitmore is expecting us."

The butler guided them to the drawing room. It looked much like Hartigan House's drawing room had before Ginger had redecorated—locked in the Victorian age. However, there was not a speck of dust to be found and the room glowed in soft candlelight.

Lady Whitmore rose to greet them. "Please be seated. Maurice has provided tea and biscuits." The lady poured three cups.

"Sugar?"

Basil nodded. Ginger declined.

"Nothing like a good cup of tea in such dreary weather as this," Lady Whitmore said.

"Is Lord Whitmore at home?" Ginger asked.

Lady Whitmore clucked. "No. The silly man's gone fishing at Canvey Island. In this weather! I do hope the old goat doesn't drown."

She laughed at her own attempt at humour and sipped her tea.

Basil ate a biscuit and complimented his hostess on it.

"Jones is a terrific baker. And cook, too. We are so fortunate to have her."

"Having a good cook is key to a happy household, isn't it?" Ginger said agreeably.

"Indeed."

Basil wiped the crumbs that had fallen on his lap into his palm and onto a small plate.

"I see you are feeling better?" Ginger said.

"Yes, quite," Lady Whitmore said lightly. "A slight case of the flu. I hope no one else was unwell?"

"Princess Sophia had also felt unwell." Ginger wondered if perhaps the women had succumbed to something more sinister than influenza.

"Lady Whitmore, we believe you have information that will help us," Basil said.

"Well, I can't be certain of that." Lady Whitmore sipped her tea. "I'm sure murder is a complicated affair, but one never knows, does one?"

"The small clue often unlocks a case," Basil said. "So, what do you have?"

Lady Whitmore leaned in eagerly, clearly enjoying her moment in Basil's spotlight.

"The *Blue Desire* the grand duchess was wearing was a fake."

Ginger and Basil shared a quick look of disappointment. This wasn't news.

Lady Whitmore continued, "I know it's common practice not to wear overly expensive jewellery when out in a public place, but I have it on good authority that even the fake blue diamond worn by the grand duchess didn't belong to her."

"To whom did it belong?"

"Well, that I don't know, Chief Inspector."

"How does your source know this?" Ginger asked.

"Oh, well, she got it on good authority too." She smiled widely. "More tea?"

"Do you mind if we stop at Hartigan House?" Ginger asked. "There is something I need to quickly grab."

"Certainly."

"I should've just driven here myself, save you having to drive me all the way back to Regent Street. In fact, that's too much out of the way. I can take a taxicab when I'm ready."

"I don't mind waiting, Ginger."

The way he said her name made her knees soften. She didn't have the energy to refute him right now, so instead turned to the gate of her home. The front door was unlocked, and he followed her inside.

"Please make yourself comfortable in the sitting room," Ginger said. He'd often been to Hartigan House and knew the way.

She hurried upstairs and only when she closed the doors behind her did she let out her breath. Boss' black and white head bobbed up in greeting.

"Oh, Boss." She scrubbed him behind the ears and kissed his forehead. "It's so easy being a dog. No puzzles to solve, no matters of the heart to plague you."

Ginger didn't *really* need to grab anything, only her sound mind. She removed her shoes and stretched out her toes before putting them back on. A cursory check in the long mirror assured her the seams of her stockings were straight. She brushed her bob and reinforced the red curls that rested on her cheeks. She touched up her makeup and dabbed on her perfume.

Oh, mercy! Why had she done that?

For professionalism, of course. It had nothing to do with the handsome man whose mere presence caused her chest to ache.

She scooped up Boss and gave him a playful squeeze before returning him to his spot at the foot of her bed. "If only men were as loyal and uncomplicated as you."

Having kept the chief inspector waiting long enough, she entered the sitting room. "So sorry for keeping you waiting."

Basil stood. "I didn't even notice the time. It gave me a chance to think about the case."

"And?"

"Still nothing."

"Ginger, is that you?" Felicia entered the room with dramatization fit for the stage. "Oh, hello, Chief Inspector. Ginger, do you have any news about Angus?" As of late, when seeing Ginger, her only inquiry was about Angus Green.

"I'm sorry, Felicia, no. But I went to see his father this morning, and he seems unconcerned."

"Are you enquiring about Mr. Angus Green?" Basil asked.

"Yes," Felicia said. "He's part of my acting company. Have you news?"

"I'm aware of his case, though I don't handle missing persons myself. I do know that as of this morning there had been no word."

Felicia collapsed in a chair. "Oh dear."

"I'm sure he's all right," Basil said. "Young men, especially of means, are often in the habit of doing what they want, when they want, without thinking about the effect it has on others."

Felicia crossed her arms, the bell-sleeves of her rayon blouse hanging from slender wrists. "You discredit my class, Chief Inspector."

"It's my class, too, actually," Basil responded. "And unfortunately true. If Mr. Green wanted to make himself scarce, there are plenty of ways to do it if you have connections and resources."

"But why would he? We had two shows left."

"Perhaps he got himself into a pickle and decided to lie low," Ginger said. "A gambling debt perhaps."

"Or was caught in an illicit affair," Basil added.

Felicia blushed at the connotation.

Basil considered her apologetically. "It's not unheard of."

"Felicia darling, I hate to say this, but it looks like Mr.

Green doesn't want to be found," Ginger said. "At any rate, I'm not the right person for this job. I'm much too busy now with a murder having just occurred in my shop."

Felicia pouted. "I just can't believe he'd leave without saying anything to me."

Ginger didn't say it, as her poor younger sister-in-law was clearly finding out for herself—men could be rascals.

"The police are still on it," Ginger said. "If there's something to be found regarding Mr. Green, they shall find it."

Felicia looked disappointed but not overly distressed. She sighed, then put a record on the gramophone and curled up by the fireplace with a book.

"Shall we depart?" Basil said with a nod toward the door.

"Do you mind if I bring Boss?" Ginger said. "I promise, he'll be especially well behaved."

Basil looked less than enthused at her request. Ginger was aware of Basil's dislike of animals of the canine variety. She still hoped little Boss would win him over.

"It's only a short trip to my motorcar," she said in an effort to encourage him.

Basil relented. "Very well."

As she promised, Boss remained on his best behaviour, sitting obediently by her feet.

Only the rumble of the Austin's engine invaded the silence between Ginger and Basil as he motored down West Carriage Drive through Hyde Park with its brown, wet lawns and naked trees, and then east towards

Feathers & Flair. Not even the case produced enough fodder to keep a natural conversation going.

Ginger attempted to climb the invisible wall that had grown between them. "If the strass stone that was stolen from Olga Pavlovna's neck didn't belong to her, then who did it belong to?"

"That's a good question," Basil said, keeping his eyes on the road. "No report of theft or missing jewels has come in."

"I would be surprised if there were. Though pastes are common, no one of good breeding would admit to having them, much less wearing them. Unless news of the loss hits the gossip rounds, it's quite a dead end."

"Are there no other gossips, other than Lady Whitmore?"

Ginger was about to shake her head, but then she thought of Mrs. Schofield. "Perhaps. Let me think about it and I'll let you know."

CHAPTER TWELVE

*G*inger briefly checked in with Madame Roux before driving off in the Daimler alone with Boss. The gears of the old motorcar stuttered as she moved them about, having to speed up and slow down as one did in London. Within minutes she arrived at her destination—St. George's City of London.

"We're here, Boss."

Reverend Oliver Hill greeted her warmly.

"Lady Gold. A pleasure as always." Their voices bounced off the stone walls and floated up along the high ceilings. He patted Boss on the head. "Hello, young pup."

Ginger put Boss on the floor and commanded him to sit. Boss did as instructed, though his stubby tail refused to still.

"Had I known you were coming," the reverend said, "I'd have had Mrs. Davies prepare tea."

"It was an impulsive decision," Ginger returned. Basil had nothing to do with her being here.

She was getting quite good at lying to herself.

"You're always welcome, I hope you know. I do hope you count me as a friend."

"I do Rev—"

"Please call me, Oliver."

"All right, Oliver. You may call me Ginger."

"Ginger? My belief is that your Christian name is Georgia."

"That's correct. Georgia after my father, George." Georgia Hartigan was the name on her birth certificate and London her place of birth. Despite growing up in Boston, Massachusetts, Ginger felt intrinsically English.

She pointed to her hair. "But my mother dubbed me Ginger, and it stuck."

Oliver laughed. "My brothers call me Carrot. Ginger is much nicer."

Ginger laughed along.

"I do view you as a friend, Oliver. Even though I've been living in London for half a year, I find I haven't made many. There's Haley, of course, Miss Higgins, but I brought her with me." Ginger chuckled. "So she doesn't count as new."

"I'm honoured to have made your list. I'm certain it won't be a short one for long."

"Well, I am quite busy with my shop and not entirely available. One must be a friend to make a friend, as they say."

"Let's go into the kitchen," Oliver said. "I'm quite capable of making a pot of tea."

"Do you mind if Boss comes?"

"Not at all. I'm a dog lover myself. Sadly, I'm too busy

with my parishioners to give a dog the proper attention he'd deserve to own one myself."

Ginger and Boss followed Oliver to the church kitchen, Ginger glimpsing the elaborate stained-glass window behind the pulpit, the daylight piercing the primary colours—red, yellow and blue—which made up images of Jesus and the saints.

The kitchen was simple in its design and wares. Oliver took her jacket and Ginger claimed a chair at the table. She instructed Boss to sit at her feet.

Oliver whistled as he worked and before long the tea was ready. He even provided a few packaged biscuits. "Not as good as homemade," he said, "but they do in a pinch."

Ginger found Oliver's openness refreshing. "How long have you been vicar at St. George's?" She'd only known the reverend for two months and their conversations always had to do with the needs of London's less fortunate and the start-up of the Child Wellness Project.

"Three years. I came from Canterbury. Took over the parish when Reverend Wood retired."

Since they'd declared themselves friendly, she thought she could ask a more intimate question. "Why haven't you married?"

Oliver had just taken a sip of tea and choked a little.

"I'm sorry. Is that too personal?"

"No, it's fine. Actually, my marital status is of a great concern to the parishioners of St. George's. The female population that is."

Ginger laughed. "I can see why. You'd be a fine catch! What's preventing a match?"

Oliver paused, caught her eye and said with meaning, "Well, I haven't met quite the right lady yet."

"Oh." The air around them grew thick with increasing discomfiture. Ginger considered herself to be astute, yet the reverend's now-apparent affection for her caught her by surprise. Oliver Hill had a friendly face, a childlike demeanour as if he'd been sheltered from the evil of the world, a wholesomeness she wasn't used to seeing in men. Though she liked the vicar, she'd never considered him anything more than a friend.

He wasn't anything like the adventurous Daniel or the serious Basil.

Ginger considered herself a modern woman and not one to let the traditions of the well-entrenched class system guide her heart. Still, she couldn't see herself as the wife of a vicar, and marriage was where any relationship would lead, should it grow serious.

Oliver looked stricken at his blunder and his right eye began to twitch. "I'm sorry, I've embarrassed you."

"No, no. It's fine. My mind just . . . Well . . ."

Oliver's face flushed deep red. "Please, just forget I said anything."

Oh, mercy. They were trapped in a cycle of apologies and unease.

"So, the Elliot cousins," Oliver started, sounding desperate to change the subject. "I'm afraid I haven't seen them since you were here last. I'm a bit worried about them, actually."

"Oh?" Ginger said, relieved to be off that last topic, but now experiencing a prickle of concern over the boys. "Why's that?"

"They're kind of on their own now that their uncle's dead."

"He died? Scout never mentioned anything." But then again, when would he have?

"Just after Christmas. We had a small funeral for him here."

Ginger sighed. "I wish I'd known."

"I would've contacted you had I been aware of your friendship with the lads."

"Are they living in the same place?"

"I believe so."

"Do you have an address?"

"Yes. It's in the office. I'll get it."

As Ginger waited whilst sipping her tea, her mind reverted to other troubling thoughts: A dead grand duchess and a murderer on the loose; Felicia's missing friend; Poor orphaned Scout and Marvin; Basil's *choice*; Oliver's kindness and his misplaced affection for her.

She wasn't sure which was most concerning.

Oliver bounded into the kitchen, apparently recovered, with a small piece of paper in his hand. "This is their address. Of course, there's no telephone number."

"Thank you." Ginger stood to receive the note. "I'm going to see if I can find them straightaway."

Oliver ducked to look into her eyes, a move that made Ginger's heart skip a beat. His blue-green eyes had flecks of gold in them—she hadn't noticed that before—and were filled with tenderness. Perhaps she'd been too quick to discard his affection?

Oliver tilted his head when he spoke. "I hope I didn't harm our friendship in anyway with my—"

"Certainly not," Ginger replied quickly. "You have been a tremendous source of comfort and good advice and I'll always treasure our friendship."

"Terrific." Oliver straightened and shoved his fists into his trouser pockets. "So good of you to drop in. The Elliot boys are blessed to have you as their 'guardian angel.'"

"The blessing runs both ways. Please do let me know if one of them ever finds himself in trouble."

Oliver helped her into her fur-trimmed coat. "Of course."

Ginger tightened the coat around her waist, tugged on her gloves, and then smiled up at Oliver."

"Thank you for the tea."

"You're most welcome."

Ginger patted her leg and called Boss to her side.

Oliver walked them to the side entrance of the kitchen. "Take good care, Ginger."

"And you too, Oliver." Ginger shook his hand before climbing into her motorcar. Boss took his position on the passenger side.

Ginger's experience driving on the left was limited, with her default naturally veering right when her mind wasn't fully engaged. It was only the loud blaring of a motorcar horn that alerted her to the fact she'd crossed the middle line. She pulled sharply on the steering wheel, just in time. Her heart raced at the near miss. Forcing herself to focus on the road, she tightly gripped the steering wheel.

She parked on the opposite side of the road from Scout and Marvin's home, staring at the dilapidated place. Despair drizzled over her.

"Oh, Scout."

Ginger knocked on the door. When no one answered, she knocked again. Were the boys out? If so, where did they go? She was relatively certain they didn't go to school. Her heart tugged at the dim prospects for their future. She wanted to help, but so far, they had rejected her offers. She'd even once invited Scout to move in with her, but he'd declined—although that was when his uncle was still alive. Apart from Marvin, Scout had no family that she knew of.

"Scout?" Ginger shouted loudly. The door wasn't so solid that it would keep her voice out. "It's Mrs. Gold." Boss, on his leash, whimpered at her side.

When Ginger had met young Scout on the SS *Rosa*, she hadn't yet pulled out her title which she'd never used in Boston, and Scout knew her as Mrs. Gold.

The lock unlatched, and Scout's nose appeared through the crack. "Dat yer, missus?"

"It is. May I come in?"

Scout nervously glanced about himself.

"It's all right, Scout. You're allowed to let friends come inside."

"It's a mite messy, missus."

"I promise I won't look."

Scout opened the door to let her in. The living space was as unkempt as the outside. The place was small and dirty. It smelled of mould and dust mites and the scent of sickness remained even though Mr. Elliot had been gone for a month. Dirty dishes were piled in a sink, and Ginger wondered if they even had running water. She could hear the high-pitched screeching of mice and rats inside the walls. Ginger pretended not to notice.

"Yer brought Boss!" Scout fell to the dirty floor and hugged the small dog. Boss greeted the boy with plenty of wet kisses.

"He 'members me."

"Of course he does."

Scout, recalling his manners, stood and stared up at Ginger. "'ow can I 'elp yer, missus?"

"I want to see how you are, Scout. I didn't know your uncle had passed away."

Scout's gaze fell to his feet. He shuffled his scuffed-up leather shoes which had a hole in the right toe. "T'is sad. But Marvin and me do well enough."

"Enough to manage the rent?"

"Me and Marvin find work to pay it."

"How is your landlord?"

Scout stared at his feet, avoiding Ginger's eyes.

"'e's all right."

Ginger sensed that Scout was shielding the man. Landlords in this sort of area had a reputation for being nasty.

"Are you going to school?"

Scout puckered his face. "Nah. Don't like no book learnin'."

"But . . ." Ginger let her objections lie. She'd have this conversation with Marvin. He was operating as Scout's guardian now.

"Scout, love, you could come and live with me." Ginger said. "You'd be safe and warm and always have enough to eat."

"Would I 'ave to 'ave a barf?"

Ginger couldn't help but chuckle at the lad's disinclination to bathe. "Once in a while, love."

"Nah, missus. I couldn't leave Marvin. He needs me."

"Oh, child." Though it was disheartening, Scout was better off here than in the workhouse. She wished she could just pluck the boy out of this heap of despair, even against his will.

However, if she did that he'd be angry and possibly turn against her. Besides, she wasn't home enough. She felt guilty leaving Boss behind when she did. She surely wasn't prepared to be a parent of a wayward child.

Scout, so intuitive for one so young, smiled his crooked-tooth smile. "I'll be all right, missus. Yer dun 'ave to worry about me."

Ginger hated to leave Scout alone. A sweet boy like that should have a mother and father, not be brought up by other children.

"Are yer still looking for the actor?" Scout said, his little face crumpling. "Cuz we 'aven't seen 'im. None about 'ere 'ave seen 'im."

"Oh, I'd forgotten I'd asked you to keep a lookout for him. It's not necessary any longer."

"Did yer find the chap?"

"I stopped looking."

Scout's young face twisted in distress. "Does that mean yer wanchyer money back?"

"Dear me, no. I asked you to do that for me. It's yours."

Relief crossed Scout's face, and Ginger's heart squeezed with pity for the child. So many burdens for one so young. Ginger had to hold herself back from grabbing him and making a run for it.

"When will Marvin get in?" she asked.

"Dunno, missus."

"If you're ever in trouble, just find a policeman and tell him to ring me, okay?"

"I will, missus."

Ginger tugged on Boss's leash and made for the door. "I have to go now, Scout. Remember what I said. Goodbye."

Scout shot towards Boss to give him one last scrub about the ears. "Good-bye old chum."

Ginger started the Daimler and puttered down the road. Ahead she saw a group of older boys, one of them familiar. Marvin.

Ginger feared they were up to no good, and when Marvin spotted Ginger, his eyes widened in recognition. Instead of approaching to greet her, he said something to the other lads, and they took off like a shot between the terraced houses.

Oh dear, what was that boy up to?

She slowed to a stop, rolled down her window, and shouted, "Marvin!"

Waiting, she wondered if she should chase after him, but a glance at her pointy-toed shoes with two-inch heels told her the idea was foolhardy.

CHAPTER THIRTEEN

*G*inger returned to Feathers & Flair to borrow the paper easel from the design room. Madame Roux reassured her that she was perfectly capable of closing the shop at the end of the day. Everything was running fine—"No dead bodies today," she quipped. Ginger had to wonder if that now defined a good day.

Back at Hartigan House, Ginger set up the easel near the fireplace. Lizzie produced tea and offered an update on the affairs of the house.

"The dowager Lady Gold has retired early, Miss Higgins' has yet to return from the medical school, and Miss Gold has gone out."

"Out?"

"She didn't say where, madam, but one of her acting companions picked her up."

"What did he look like?"

"About your height, I suppose, light brown hair, specs, and a moustache."

"That sounds like Mr. Haines."

"That's it. I heard Miss Gold say his name."

"Did Miss Gold say what she was doing?"

"Just that they were going to the theatre to prepare for auditions."

Ginger sat in her favourite chair, the one closest to the hearth, and patted her leg for Boss to jump up. They both settled in comfortably as she sipped her tea and stared at the blank page.

Once her tea had cooled, she shifted Boss to the side and picked up a pencil. She drew a circle in the middle and labeled it "Grand Duchess" and under that in small cursive, *Russian refugee*.

She added six spokes of a wheel, drawing circles at the end of each and filled them in: Lady Ilsa Lyon, *kleptomaniac;* husband Lord Lyon, *protective;* Princess Sophia, *territorial enemies*; Lord Whitmore, *British secret service agent*; Countess Andreea Balcescu, *elusive*.

Perhaps Ginger's intuition about Lady Lyon was misguided. Could the lady have been so desperate for the *Blue Desire*, she'd break the duchess' neck to get it? Ginger had a hard time picturing the delicate-looking lady managing such a violent act and succeeding with the grand duchess who had appeared to be rather strong. Perhaps her husband completed the death act to protect his wife.

Or was Princess von Altenhofen really a German agent who'd had dealings in Russia that the grand duchess knew about? Dangerous secrets she couldn't risk falling into the hands of the British? Would she fake an illness to avoid suspicion? Then what of Lady Whitmore's ailment? Perhaps the princess dropped something into Lady Whitmore's tea, giving her own fainting spell credence?

Had Lord Whitmore been afraid of the same thing? Only the other way around? Dangerous secrets couldn't risk falling into the hands of the Russians?

And how did the Romanian countess fit in? Ginger would've dismissed her from the suspect list if the lady hadn't turned into a ghost.

Whatever was going on, Ginger had the feeling it had to do with a lot more than a jewel theft.

She replayed the events of the evening in her mind. Ginger had been attuned to everything that went on, running on adrenaline, excited for the gala and wanting everyone to have a good time. Her eyes had continually scanned the guests, her ears capturing their conversations —did they like what they saw there? Was Feathers & Flair everything the gossips and advertisers had said it would be?

She wrinkled her nose and added another spoke to the chart. In the circle, she wrote Lady Fitzhugh and Meredith Fitzhugh. As much as Ginger hated to consider poor, beaten-down Meredith, the hatred she'd seen in the girl's eyes for beautiful Olga Pavlovna had been unmistakable. Meredith was a hefty girl with large hands. She added in cursive, *jealousy*.

Ginger settled back into her chair and Boss returned to her lap. He circled once before curling up. Ginger continued to stare at the board. What was she missing?

The doorbell rang, and Ginger heard the murmur of Pippins's voice when he answered it, not loud enough, though, to make out who he'd invited in. The older man opened the door to the sitting room and announced:

"Chief Inspector Reed."

Ginger was about to push Boss off her lap when Basil stopped her.

"Please, not on my account."

"Very well," Ginger said. "Would you like a drink?"

"Actually, I'd like that very much."

"Pips, would you be a dear and get the chief inspector a gin and tonic." Ginger knew the chief inspector's drink of choice from their previous engagements.

The butler nodded. "Anything for you, madam?"

"A glass of wine, if you please."

"Certainly, madam," Pippins replied.

Basil's attention was on the easel, his expression a mix of surprise and admiration.

"I see you've been busy," he said.

"Yes, well, I don't know that I've made any progress." Her hands were bare and she played with her jade glass ring. A gift from her father, it had a floral pattern imprinted on the stone with a gold setting encircled with tiny inset diamonds.

"Everything is such a muddle," Ginger continued. "Everyone had means and opportunity. But what of motive?"

Pippins brought the drinks and politely left them alone.

"A public place like your dress shop makes it virtually impossible to narrow down fingerprints, and with an unregistered event like the gala, it really could be anyone

—a madman, or lady, off the street. I confess, Scotland Yard is drawing a blank."

"No luck with the code, then?" Ginger asked.

"Not so far. We can't even be sure it has anything to do with the crime. It could be entirely unrelated."

Ginger nodded but didn't believe it to be true. Not with Lord Whitmore and so many international guests present. She moved Boss to the floor and he moved to his favourite spot on the carpet in front of the hearth.

Ginger produced her copy of the code and wrote it out on the board: W533o 8h 849h 975 wt90 @$.

"Could W mean weight?" Basil said. "H meaning height, T for time? Perhaps a bomb drop?"

"Let's hope not! Did we not just fight the war to end all wars?"

Basil shrugged.

"Perhaps the letters represent numbers and numbers letters," Ginger said. "So 'W' would be 23." She wrote the number under the letter. "533 would be Ecc, and 'o' would be 15."

"A Bible verse?" Basil said. "Ecc is the abbreviation for Ecclesiastes. Do you have a Bible nearby?"

"With only twelve chapters, it would have to be from the apocryphal book of Ecclesiasticus." Ginger pointed to the bookshelf. "There's a Bible with the Apocrypha on the bottom right."

Basil retrieved the thick, leather-bound book and thumbed through it.

"Ecclesiastes 23:15. The man that is accustomed to opprobrious words will never be reformed all the days of his life."

Ginger's forehead crumpled. "Opprobrious words."

"Expressing scorn or criticism."

"What could it mean?" Ginger asked. "Do you think it's referring to a specific person?"

"I don't know."

"The word 'reform' possibly refers to the revolution in Russia." Ginger said. "It was a Russian aristocrat that was killed."

"Let's go with that theory. Who would've benefited by receiving this message? Who would want to send it?"

Ginger stared at the easel again.

"We're forgetting about the rest of the code. Applying the same system, we get nothing. 8h would be H8. 849h is Hdl8. Doesn't make sense."

Basil emptied his glass and set it on the sideboard. He turned, his hazel eyes boring into hers.

"Ginger."

Ginger stilled, dread creeping through her as she guessed at what Basil was about to say.

"It's not necessary," she said softly.

"I daresay it is. I know you don't want to talk about it, but I must. I know I've wronged you. I've led you to believe I cared about you beyond our burgeoning friendship and that's because I *do* care about you. I wasn't trifling with your feelings. I'd never do that."

"You're interested in me?"

"Yes."

"But?" If Basil's wife had not been unfaithful, if he hadn't been separated from his wife for as long as he had, Ginger would never have opened her heart to him.

Basil emitted a heavy sigh. "Emelia is my wife. She's

begged my forgiveness. We've been married for *eleven* years. I'm compelled to give it another try."

Pain squeezed Ginger's heart. This was her own fault. Despite his indication that a divorce was imminent, Basil *was* married. She'd known that.

And she respected how he wanted to honour his vows.

"It's fine," Ginger said, forcing a smile. "I understand."

Basil dipped his chin. "I should go."

Ginger walked Basil through the entrance hall. "We can be good friends." She extended her hand, a peace offering, and Basil took it, relief spreading across his face.

"Friends."

CHAPTER FOURTEEN

When Haley returned home from her day of classes, Ginger poured them both a sherry and offered a crystal glass to Haley when she entered the sitting room.

Haley took the glass and sipped before collapsing on the settee. She watched Ginger curiously. "Hard day?"

"Interesting day." Ginger relayed the time she and Basil had spent interviewing Lady Lyon and Princess Altenhofen, and his most recent visit, but excluding his declaration of affection. Some things were personal and meant to be held close to the chest.

"I'm very concerned about Scout," she said when she got to that part of her narrative.

Haley commiserated. "At least he has you and the work you're doing with Reverend Hill."

Ginger flushed at the memory of *that* awkward moment. Today was apparently the day for declarations. She sipped her sherry before Haley could intuit anything.

Haley nodded towards the easel. "Did your graph help?"

"Not so far. It's a very troubling case."

Haley crossed her legs, pulling at the hosiery that had twisted at her ankles. "Certainly not cut-and-dried," she said.

Ginger held a palm to her lips in an effort to hold in a yawn. She felt emotionally and physically exhausted. "Anyway, enough about me. How was your day?"

"Lectures mostly."

"Boring?"

"Nothing about medicine is boring to me," Haley said, brightening at the change of topic. "Only, I'm happiest when I can get my hands dirty. Get in there with a scalpel."

"I suppose Dr. Watts isn't calling on you to assist him so much now that Dr. Gupta is here."

"Dr. Watts favours Dr. Gupta, of course. I miss being his first in line."

"I guess you'll have to become Dr. Gupta's first in line."

Haley stared into space. "You might be right."

Ginger giggled and Haley scowled. "For the sake of my education, Ginger, that's all."

With a twinkle in her eye Ginger answered, "I didn't mean to imply anything else."

"About your case," Haley said, changing the subject. "Have you and the chief inspector a theory as to why two women at your gala had fainting fits?"

"Lady Whitmore claims it was the flu, but Princess Sophia has made no comment. Originally, I believed it was coincidental to the grand duchess' demise, but now I'm not so sure."

"What changed your mind?"

"I've had time to ponder." Ginger tapped at her lips with her well-manicured fingernail. "Both incidences made opportunity for someone to sneak upstairs unseen."

"Maybe the grand duchess dropped something in Princess Sophia's drink to create a diversion," Haley said. "It was clear she and the princess didn't care for one another, so if it didn't matter who the grand duchess chose, then why not someone she disliked?"

"Exactly. But if the grand duchess delivered her shawl upstairs at that time why the second victim? Why Lady Whitmore?"

Haley pressed her lips together. "I'm not sure."

"Perhaps there was a second person in need of a different kind of diversion. Lady Whitmore's sudden malady prevented Lord Whitmore from going upstairs to retrieve the shawl."

Haley rested her glass on her lap and nodded. "Someone besides yourself knew Lord Whitmore works for the British secret service."

"It's a possibility."

Voices echoed through the foyer and Felicia burst into the sitting room. She'd brought one of the other gentleman actors home, Matthew Haines, the fellow who played the detective in *Sham*.

"Oh, Mr. Haines," Ginger said. "Hello."

Matthew Haines's eyes were on the easel and Ginger quickly rose, positioning herself to block his view. "Would you like a drink?" she asked lightly.

Matthew glanced at Felicia and she nodded.

"I can get it," Felicia said. "What would you like?" Matthew followed Felicia to the sideboard, and Ginger took that moment to rip the page off the easel, fold it twice and slip it under her chair. Haley watched with approval.

Felicia and Matthew joined them, drinks in hand. Ginger noted that Matthew held his drink in his left hand.

"Are you from London?" she asked. She suspected not, but she couldn't quite place his accent.

"No, I'm an immigrant. Russian, actually. Not something I like to advertise, under the current politic climate."

"Matthew and Haines are English names," Ginger said.

"My mother is Russian. She calls me Matvei. My stepfather is as English as they come."

Boss moseyed over and hopped onto Ginger's lap. "Mr. Haines, what do you know about the grand duchess?"

Matthew Haines raised a shoulder. "I never had much to do with the Russian aristocracy, and they're always breeding with you lot—no offence, Lady Gold. I'm just a simple bloke working for my next meal."

"I see." Ginger turned her attention to Felicia who seemed in bright spirits. She crossed her legs, bouncing the top one as she'd been known to do when she was looking for attention from the opposite sex. As usual, it worked this time too, and Matthew was quite mesmerized by Felicia's shapely calf.

Ginger cleared her throat, gaining Felicia's attention. "And what are your plans now?"

"Now that Mr. McGuire has to drop *Sham*," Felicia

117

said, "the director is opening early auditions for the next play. Mr. Haines and I are going to learn our lines. I've decided to audition for the role of the leading lady."

Matthew rubbed his moustache and pushed up on his spectacles. He grinned at Felicia mischievously. "What if I want to audition for the leading lady?"

Felicia giggled. "Don't be ridiculous."

"Why not? Men played the female roles during Shakespeare's time." Matthew jumped to his feet and plucked Felicia's discarded shawl and cloche from a chair. He tied the shawl around his waist like a skirt and stuck the hat on his head.

"Mr. Haines!" Felicia declared. The sitting room filled with the ripple of her laughter.

"I'm Mrs. Plum," Matthew said with a convincing falsetto. "I'm here to steal the leading lady role from you."

Felicia played along. "I expect your moustache may be a problem, madam."

Matthew stroked his upper lip. "Oh yes. This unfortunate creature is hereditary. My grandmother knitted a scarf after shaving hers off."

Felicia roared with laughter as Matthew removed his props.

Ginger and Haley applauded the short performance. "Well done, Mr. Haines."

Matthew bowed.

"Felicia, you'd better start practicing if you hope for a chance to win this part," Ginger said.

Felicia giggled. "Apparently!"

"Would you like to use this room?" Ginger offered.

Felicia was on her feet collecting her things. "No, we

shall use the drawing room. The acoustics are better there."

Matthew finished his drink and set his empty tumbler on the table. It was then that Ginger noticed scratches on Matthew's hands."

"Run-in with a cat?" Ginger said with a smile as she pointed a long fingernail in Matthew's direction. Matthew made a show of examining his wounds.

"Nah, that's from my ineffectual offer to help one of the stage hands shift a backdrop around. Deuced thing ended up hitting the floor. Good intentions, though, you know."

Felicia and Matthew left in good humour.

Haley raised a dark brow. "That was quite the show."

"Felicia seems to be taken with Mr. Haines," Ginger said, frowning. Felicia had fallen into the habit of playing with men's feelings—a cycle of flirting, dating, then growing bored, and often leaving a forlorn man in her wake. She wondered how long before Mr. Haines would be crying in his soup.

CHAPTER FIFTEEN

*P*ippins tapped on the frame of the morning room door. "Madam, a gentleman is here to see you."

Ginger's heart did a small somersault. *Was it Basil?* And blast him for making her heart jump!

Pippins continued. "A Superintendent Morris, madam. From the Yard. He'd like to see Miss Higgins, as well."

Haley shot Ginger a look before wiping her wide mouth with a linen serviette and followed her to the sitting room. Boss scampered after them.

Ginger hadn't met Superintendent Morris, had only heard about him briefly from Basil. Whenever Morris's name came up, Basil was always keen to move off the topic.

"What a surprise, Superintendent," Ginger said as he entered the sitting room. The man was oversized in height and girth. His trench coat pinched at his armpits and opened to reveal a waistcoat with buttons that looked like they were about to pop. She shook his hand. "Please have a seat."

"No, no, no, I'll stand if you don't mind." The superintendent turned to Haley. "And you must be Miss Higgins? I'm assuming because of your studious costume and your age." He nodded as if he'd just performed a magic trick, displaying his gift of deduction.

Haley looked affronted and didn't offer a reply.

The superintendent's gaze moved around the room resting momentarily on the *Mermaid* painting above the hearth. All men did this when they first entered the sitting room. The superintendent's brow wrinkled when his eyes found the blank easel in the corner, and Ginger was glad she'd removed her investigation sketch.

Ginger and Haley sat, and Ginger motioned to the superintendent. "Please have a seat."

"I'll stand if that is all right with you."

"If that's what you prefer. How may we help you?"

"Yes, yes, yes," the superintendent said. "Let me see. You were at the event at, what is it . . . ?" He flipped through his notebook, "Yes, Feathers & Flair." He laughed. "At first I thought it was a shop for shooting sports."

Ginger frowned.

"You were there?" Superintendent Morris repeated.

"Yes, of course. It's my shop. I planned and promoted the event."

"And Miss Higgins, you were there also?"

Haley was on record with the police as being in attendance. She scowled at the superintendent. "I was."

Morris swivelled to face Ginger. "Lady Gold, how was

it that certain members of the public came to be in attendance?"

"Through personal and public invitation," Ginger said. "We advertised the gala at the shop."

"I see. So you didn't know the grand duchess?"

"No. I met her for the first time at my event."

The man paced the Persian carpet. Boss looked up from his spot by the fireplace and let out a low growl. Morris continued, "Miss Higgins, would you also say you didn't know the grand duchess or a lady known as Mary Parker?"

Haley shook her head. "No. Is that her real name? Why would you think I might know her?"

"She's spent some time in America."

"I spent twenty years in America," Ginger said. "I've never heard the name before."

Morris placed a thick finger to his lips. "Right, right, right." He spun on his heel mid-pace and narrowed his eyes at Ginger. "Of course, you wouldn't be likely to tell me the truth, would you, Mrs. Gold?"

Ginger was quick to note how Morris dropped her title. She stared back sternly. "And why would I not tell you the truth?"

"Is it true you spent time in France during the war?"

"Yes," Ginger said. "Both Miss Higgins and I did. She as a nurse, and I was a telephone operator."

Morris scoffed. "A nurse and a telephone operator?"

"Yes. What is so funny about that?"

"Let's say, for the sake of form, that it was true. Where you not both in Beauvais, France during the same week?"

Haley furrowed her brow. "We met there briefly.

Forgive me, but what are you trying to get at?"

Ginger's feathers were ruffled. After the war, she had signed the Official Secrets Act. She was forbidden by law to discuss the details of that time with *anyone*. Not even Haley, whom she trusted implicitly, and quite honestly, that restriction grieved her. There were times when she *longed* to talk about the part she had played in the war. If only she could speak about it, she might feel some relief, might be able to fulfill some sort of penance, some sort of absolution. As it was, she was yoked to her secrets—an unbearable sentence on most days. This was why she worked so hard to forget. Keep as busy as possible with work at the shop, find a diversion in solving puzzles that will bring wicked people to justice. Stay "happy" to spread happiness.

Morris was about to break that law for her.

"Superintendent Morris," she said sharply. "I don't know what you're talking about, and I'm *certain* Miss Higgins doesn't." She hoped Morris would pick up on her meaning, but somehow she doubted this bluff fellow was intuitive enough. A sideways glance at Haley told Ginger that she *had* got the message.

"Right, right, right." Morris blundered on. "I understand you're not permitted to speak of it. Did you meet Mary Parker in France?"

"*Who* is Mary Parker?" Ginger asked.

"The alias of Grand Duchess Olga Pavlovna Orlova."

Ginger and Haley shared a look. Why hadn't Basil informed Ginger of this new information? She questioned the superintendent. "Does Chief Inspector Reed know you're here?"

"I do not answer to Chief Inspector Reed. In fact, it is the other way around. Now, please answer the question."

"I did not meet a lady of that name in France," Ginger stated.

"Neither did I," Haley said. "Why? Was she there?"

"She was, Miss Higgins. She was there in the same capacity as I believe you and Mrs. Gold were. Miss Parker worked for MI5. She also worked for the Kremlin."

Ginger huffed at the man's bull-headedness.

"What are you saying, Superintendent Morris?" Haley asked.

"I'm saying Mary Parker was working for both the Russian government and the British."

Ginger didn't know why she was surprised. She'd already guessed that the grand duchess was an agent, but she hadn't suspected that the lady had been working for two sides.

"It all makes sense now," Haley muttered, her eyes latching onto Ginger. "My mysterious friend."

Ginger shrugged subtly, and offered a soft apologetic smile. Ginger's history working for the secret service during the war wasn't hers to share, though there had been a million moments when she had wanted to. Especially with Haley. And with Basil. Now that their relationship was strained, she was thankful she hadn't given in to temptation with him.

When Ginger focused back on Morris her countenance was anything but soft. His indiscretion was uncalled for.

"I think you did know Mary Parker," he continued,

"and she threatened to uncover one of your secrets Mrs. Gold, and you—"

"Broke her neck?" Ginger held up her slender fingers.

"Your gala was a terrific cover, producing a herd of suspects whilst providing none at all!"

"Superintendent Morris!" Haley sprung to her feet. "I must protest."

Morris ignored her outburst and remained focused on Ginger. He counted on three stubby fingers. "You had means, motive, and opportunity." He nearly shouted at Haley. "And so did you, Miss Higgins. Together, you could've planned this murder."

Haley, with hands on wide hips and a cutting glare, responded. "Neither Lady Gold nor I had anything to do with this."

Morris blew roughly through his dry lips. "Of course you deny it."

"You make these accusations, but you have no proof," Ginger said. "Otherwise your constables would be here with handcuffs at the ready." She stood, clasping her hands firmly in front of her dress, signalling that the interview was over, and no, she would *not* be shaking his hand.

"I'm afraid Miss Higgins and I are quite busy, so, unless you're here to arrest us, we bid you to leave."

The superintendent huffed. "As you wish. Good day, ladies." He plopped his hat on his head, spun on his heels, and left without another word.

"Oh, can you believe the audacity of that man!" Ginger spat as she circled the sitting room to work off her extreme frustration. "Positively boorish."

Haley returned to her chair and let out a long breath. "You'll get no argument from me."

Morris's indiscretion incensed Ginger. "And he, a superintendent!"

Boss glanced up at her, adding a low growl of support.

"There are bad eggs in every department," Haley said. "Boston, too."

Boss's little head popped up at the mention of his name.

"Indeed," Ginger said. "I fear Morris's incompetence shall impede this investigation. It's already proving to be immensely difficult."

"I'm afraid I'm going to have to let you stew in your anger alone." Haley made a show of checking her wrist-watch. "I've got a bus to catch."

"Haley," Ginger called.

"Yes?"

"What you learned about me today—I trust you'll keep it in confidence?"

Haley smiled. "Of course. You needn't have asked."

"Thank you."

Ginger had work to do too. By the time she'd dressed and driven through the city to Regent Street, her emotions had calmed. How silly for her to let that bumbling man get under her skin. She was innocent of any wrongdoing and the best way to prove that was to find the real killer.

A sense of normality had returned to Feathers & Flair. The gawkers had exhausted their visits, so most customers were legitimate in their interest to shop. Dorothy had caught her breath and no longer looked like she was about to sprint in a race, and Emma divided her time between sewing, working on designs, and helping Dorothy on the shop floor. Madame Roux attended to clients who were of the upper crust, not trusting Dorothy with astute customers and for that Ginger was grateful.

Lady Whitmore entered the shop, a gust of cold wind on her heels. Ginger was always happy to see repeat customers. "Good day, Lady Whitmore. Welcome."

"Good day to you as well, Lady Gold." Lady Whitmore appeared nervous, her eyes searching the faces of the other shoppers.

"Can I help you find something?"

"Well, no. I'll just browse if that's all right."

"Certainly. Do let me or Madame Roux know if you need any help."

Dorothy West was stationed upstairs and was more suited to assist the clientele that shopped for the factory dresses. Younger women usually, closer to her age. Ginger preferred to care for the upper classes where a particularly delicate touch was needed.

Busying herself at the cash counter, Ginger checked the register and the receipt chits. Everything seemed in order—Lady Lyon had not broken the law twice that fateful night—and once again she thanked the heavens for Madame Roux.

She turned her head in time to see Lady Whitmore creep upstairs. Ginger chuckled. More than one member of high society held a secret curiosity. One or two even purchased from the rack. Ginger often had, but she credited her learned American sensibilities when she did.

A new delivery from the milliner arrived, and Ginger

directed the deliveryman to the back of the room. He made several trips, but the fellow was genial and seemed grateful for his job.

"Ooh, I can't wait to have a look," Emma said, hurrying to be the first to open the boxes and admire the contents. Ginger was about to follow when she caught sight of Lady Whitmore sneaking downstairs. With the excitement of the new hat order arrival, Ginger had momentarily forgotten that Lady Whitmore was upstairs.

Lady Whitmore's face flushed at being spotted, and she appeared flustered.

"Is everything all right, Lady Whitmore? Was Miss West of service?"

"Yes, yes, she's fine. I, uh, just suddenly feel unwell."

Ginger called out after the lady as she bustled outside. "Take care!"

Madame Roux had witnessed the exchange.

"That was odd," Ginger said.

"Indeed. I don't think Lady Whitmore mentioned one word of gossip while she was here."

Ginger grinned. "She *really* must be feeling ill."

Dorothy joined them from upstairs.

"Lady Whitmore just did the strangest thing."

"What's that?"

"She fished through the pockets of *all* of the jackets and rummaged through the stole rack as well. Made a frightful mess, I might add."

"I wonder what she was looking for?" Madame Roux asked.

Ginger didn't answer, but she knew. Lady Whitmore had been looking for the *cigarette paper.*

CHAPTER SIXTEEN

*U*sing the directions Pippins had put together for her earlier, Ginger successfully navigated to the grand house known as Cherry Tree Manor—occupied by Lord and Lady Fitzhugh—on the outskirts of London.

It was a dominating stone structure of four stories, much of it covered in vines. A cobble-stoned drive encircled a massive fountain, turned off for the winter season. Ginger put the Daimler in park and the engine died fitfully. One day she'd trade the old girl in for something newer. Perhaps once the weather cheered.

Butlers were known to be sombre-faced and expressionless—they weren't there to be noticed or give opinions, simply to serve—but the one who opened the door of Cherry Tree Manor was particularly dour. No doubt the domineering, opinionated lady of the manor had something to do with that.

Ginger was left to wait in the entrance hall for some time, penance she thought, for not making an appointment. Eventually the butler returned and directed her to the drawing room. "Lady Gold," he announced, his face as cheerful as a thundercloud.

Lady Fitzhugh and Lady Meredith sat upright, each in one of two wingback chairs. Neither stood to greet her.

"Lady Gold," Lady Fitzhugh said. "Had we known you were coming, we would've had tea prepared."

"I'm sorry to intrude without previous notice, Lady Fitzhugh," Ginger began. "I hope you will give me a moment of your time to discuss the . . . episode . . . that transpired at Feathers & Flair."

"I wondered when someone would finally come. Where is that Chief Inspector? Why is he not with you?"

Ginger didn't want to get caught up in the reason she had chosen to come without first consulting Basil. She told herself it was because her reasons for suspecting the Fitzhughs in the first place were razor thin. Truthfully, she just didn't have the fortitude to deal with the emotional strain Basil's presence brought to her.

Besides, Basil's boss thought her a suspect. Perhaps Basil now did too?

It was a point of interest that Lady Fitzhugh expected to be included in the investigation. Then again, it would be odd if the self-important lady had not.

"Do you mind if I sit?" Ginger said.

Lady Fitzhugh waved lazily to an empty settee. "Go ahead."

Ginger had just seated herself when the door to the drawing room opened. An older gentleman stepped in halfway, then abruptly stopped. His fine suit did little to hide his ball-like girth. Square with long jowls, his face was creased by the passage of time.

"Sorry, ladies," he said, his expression almost one of fear. He quickly backed out the way he came.

"Lord Fitzhugh?" Ginger said.

Lady Fitzhugh nodded with a slight air of contempt.

Meredith Fitzhugh observed the transaction with disinterest. She'd likely seen her father scurry out of her mother's presence often. The younger lady—Ginger guessed she was in her late twenties—fussed with her shapeless dress with string sleeves, a style that unfortunately was unflattering for a girl her size. Meredith had the misfortune of getting her height from her mother and her girth from her father. She sat quite like a penguin in a golden cage, and Ginger pitied her.

Now that Ginger was sitting with the two women, she wasn't quite sure where to start. She couldn't just come out and ask if the younger lady had killed the grand duchess because of her beauty. Not only would that be offensive, it wouldn't do anything to loosen their tongues. Ginger had to approach this interview gently.

"Had either of you ever met the grand duchess before?"

The older Fitzhugh lady replied. "No. But if we had, what's it to you?"

"I'm just trying to find out what I can about the grand duchess. The smallest thing can unlock a case, you know."

"Whose case is it? *Yours?*"

"Chief Inspector Reed has asked me to . . . consult. I often accompany him on interviews."

"But not this one," she snapped.

"No. You are not a suspect Lady Fitzhugh. I've taken it upon myself to inquire of my guests, should they know anything that might help. There's really no need to be defensive."

"All right then. You've got your answer. We've never met the grand duchess, and I had never heard of her before your gala event."

"What about you, Lady Meredith? Do you know of the grand duchess Olga Pavlovna Orlova?"

Lady Meredith looked stunned at being personally addressed.

"I just said we've never heard of her," Lady Fitzhugh's eyes were narrow and her mouth a straight line.

"With all due respect, Lady Fitzhugh, you said *you*'d never heard of her. Perhaps Lady Meredith has? She's not physically attached to you, is she? She must have some other acquaintances. Perhaps one of them had mentioned the grand duchess."

Both Fitzhugh women stared back at Ginger with shocked silence, Lady Fitzhugh with disdain and Lady Meredith with something close to admiration.

"Such cheek!" Lady Fitzhugh stammered.

Ginger wasn't going to pander to Lady Fitzhugh's bad manners or sense of self-importance. She smiled pleasantly at Lady Meredith. "Have you?"

"No, Lady Gold. I have not. She was stunning though —wasn't she? Such a shame she had to die."

The way Lady Meredith admitted to this, blankly without a spark of life in her dull eyes, gave Ginger the chills.

· · ·

Ginger returned to Feathers & Flair after her disconcerting interview with the Fitzhughs. The shop was back in order, but the unrest in Ginger's chest had only grown. A lady had died and Scotland Yard was no closer to finding the culprit than before. Basil had assured her his best men were on the case, but also reminded her, with a hint of sorrow in his voice, that many murder cases grow cold, never getting solved, even ones that involved high society.

Ginger wasn't satisfied to let this one go so easily. High society was a relatively small circle. She needed to tap into the Lady Whitmores of London and discover what, if anything, Grand Duchess Olga Pavlovna Orlova had been hiding. That information could lead her to the killer. The problem was, she didn't know the "Lady Whitmores" of London, having only recently moved to the city herself.

But she did know someone who did. Mrs. Schofield.

"Madame Roux," Ginger asked during a time of calm. "You'll manage all right if I leave again, this time for the rest of the day?"

"*Mais oui*, Lady Gold. Of course."

"Terrific. I'll see you tomorrow, then."

Ginger headed back to Hartigan House and parked the Daimler in the garage. Instead of walking to the kitchen like she normally would, she cut through the path in the hedge that divided her property from Mrs. Schofield's, then circled around to the front door.

The Schofield residence was much like Hartigan House in glamour, though several square feet smaller.

Ginger used the knocker and was greeted by the Schofields' maid, Lucy.

"Hello, Lucy. Is Mrs. Schofield available?"

"Yes, madam. I'll let her know you're calling."

Ginger waited in the entrance hall only a few moments until Lucy returned.

"Mrs. Schofield is in the sitting room."

Ginger followed Lucy and joined the older lady.

"Lady Gold! What a marvellous surprise. And timely. I've just sat down for tea. Lucy, bring another teacup and a plate of sandwiches and cakes."

"Thank you for seeing me at short notice," Ginger said, sitting opposite her hostess.

"I do hope everything is all right," Mrs. Schofield said. "The dowager is well?"

"Yes, she's fine and is looking forward to your next visit." A little white lie to maintain healthy neighbourly relations didn't hurt, once in a while.

"As do I," Mrs. Schofield said. "But your grandmother is often occupied. Rather busy for a lady her age."

"Yes, well…"

Thankfully, Lucy returned with the teacups, cakes and cucumber sandwiches cut in triangles. Mrs. Schofield poured for them both.

"I know you didn't call just to see what an old lady does all day, so what can I do for you, Lady Gold?"

"That's not fair," Ginger said lightly. "I am always interested in your welfare. How is your grandson these days?"

"Alfred is fine. Still living like the war never happened, yet at the same time as if the world will end tomorrow."

She gazed at Ginger pointedly. "It would be so nice to see him with a lovely lady, a widow even, and settle down."

"Oh, well, yes, I suppose," Ginger continued quickly before her neighbour could propose another dinner invitation in order to bring Ginger and Alfred together. "Since you asked, Mrs. Schofield, I am looking for information, and I'm wondering if you could help me."

Mrs. Schofield leaned forward with interest. "Oh, do tell. What is it you want to know?"

"You've heard about the death of the Russian grand duchess Olga Pavlovna Orlova?"

"Oh yes. Quite a juicy bit of news. It happened in your dress shop, didn't it?"

"Yes. The thing is, nobody seems to know anything about her."

"And you thought that I might?"

Ginger nodded. "Yes, or perhaps you know someone who does."

"I'm quite flattered, Lady Gold, I have to say."

Ginger paused to give Mrs. Schofield time to think.

"You could ask Mrs. Needham. She's on the hospital board and knows about anyone who's ever been ill or Mrs. Silcox who chairs the Silcox Family Charity. She's quite high society." Mrs. Schofield's eyes glinted as they narrowed under folded eyelids. "Or I could just tell you."

"Please, Mrs. Schofield, if you know anything that will help the case, do tell." Besides, Ginger thought, withholding information was impeding an investigation and a crime, but she kept that bit to herself.

"Grand Duchess Olga Pavlovna is dead," Mrs. Schofield said, examining her painted nails.

"I know that."

"No, I mean, she died as a child. I don't know who died in your new shop, but it wasn't a grand duchess."

"An impostor? But how could she get into England?"

"I understand it's quite easy to forge papers these days if you know the right people."

Ginger, of all people, knew that. Whoever had created the false identity for the dead lady wasn't an amateur. It took more than luck to pass as a royal. This came from higher up the ranks.

"How did you know this, Mrs. Schofield, when Scotland Yard has yet to come to this conclusion?"

Mrs. Schofield smiled slyly. "You don't expect me to give up my sources to you?"

"Well . . ."

She laughed. "It's fine. I had a Russian-born governess as a child. She loved to teach me about her ancestral homeland. She told me all about her grand dukes and grand duchesses."

CHAPTER SEVENTEEN

*G*inger snapped the evening paper before folding it and placing it beside her dinner plate. The headline read: *WHO IS THE GRAND DUCHESS?* By Blake Brown.

Ginger stabbed his name with her polished nail. "How did he find out so quickly? I only rang Scotland Yard an hour ago."

"Perhaps the Yard was trailing the information, as well," Haley said. "That is their job after all."

"Perhaps, but I suspect Mr. Brown's contact at the Yard wasted no time in feeding him the information after it came in."

"I've noticed that you're reverting to words like 'yard' and 'station' rather than your normal usage of 'Basil.'" Haley inclined her head and said gently, "Is your friendship really that tense?"

Ginger sighed. "It's frightfully awkward. Now when we're together it's strictly business, no light bantering or joking about."

"No flirting, you mean."

"If you must be so brash, yes. No flirting. Mrs. Reed is back and even if she's not physically with us, she's *there*."

"What about this case? You're hardly leaving it to him, and I highly discourage you from making any more enquiries alone. It's just not sensible. Whoever killed the so-called grand duchess, probably wouldn't flinch at killing you—if he or she had to."

Ginger had learned a few defensive moves during the war and felt confident in her ability to ward off an attacker. But Haley was right. If the killer caught her off guard . . .

"Perhaps you should come with me, then?" Ginger said. "We're stronger as two."

"Oh, I wish I could!" Haley said. "But my studies don't allow me the time."

"Surely you have time for tea. I'm thinking a little visit to the Ritz."

"The Ritz? I don't think they'll let the likes of me in."

"Nonsense. I'll lend you an appropriate frock."

"Why would I agree? I don't even like tea, much less the company of the hoity-toity." After a pause Haley added, "Present company excluded."

Ginger ignored the jab.

"Consider it a spying operation. Part of the investigation. And cocktails instead of tea."

"Your invitation just got a lot more interesting. Who are we spying on?"

"Princess Sophia von Altenhofen."

"Why her?"

"Well, we have a grand duchess who's not really a

grand duchess, a princess who's no longer a princess, and a countess who's disappeared, seemingly into thin air."

"An aristocratic enigma."

"Since one is dead and the other can't be found . . ."

"The princess, it is." Haley stood and brushed her hands together with enthusiasm. "Where is this *appropriate* frock?"

An hour and a half later—twice as long as it should've taken according to Haley—they arrived at the Ritz hotel.

"You really do look quite becoming," Ginger said. "And I'm not the only one to think so." She nodded toward a table with two gentlemen looking their way. They each lifted a glass in acknowledgment.

"We're here to work, Ginger, not play."

"Can't one do both at the same time?"

Ginger led Haley to the same cocktail lounge she'd been to a couple of days before with Basil. Haley made clucking noises. "So this is how the other half lives."

"The London Ritz was the second hotel built by César Ritz, the Swiss hotelier. The first is in Paris."

"Looks like he's done well for himself."

"Indeed."

They selected a table with a view of the whole room, and hung their handbags over the backs of their chairs.

"What makes you think the princess will make an appearance?" Haley asked.

"Just a hunch. Princess von Altenhofen doesn't look the type to enjoy exploring London alone."

Ginger ordered a platter of cheese and crackers with caviar, and a mint jelly spread, which they enjoyed with fine French pinot noir.

Haley moaned after one bite. "This is my kind of spying operation."

Ginger toasted her. "To spies."

After another bite, Haley said, "Have you heard from Louisa, lately?"

"Yes, actually."

As a live-in nurse for the late Mr. Hartigan, Haley had become well-acquainted with Ginger's half-sister. Ginger and Louisa were ten years apart, though Louisa hardly acted her age. She'd been hopelessly spoilt by their father and by Sally, Louisa's mother and Ginger's stepmother. Motivation for moving to England included the opportunity to move out of Sally's house and Ginger suspected her stepmother was equally relieved. Despite Louisa's propensity for demanding attention by means of sulking or behaving obnoxiously, she was still Ginger's sister, and Ginger loved her.

"I received a letter from Louisa this morning," Ginger said. "I'm glad you reminded me. She sends her love."

"Staying out of trouble?"

"Well, you know Louisa. She has her own mind."

Haley spread mint jelly on a cracker. "I kind of miss her antics, though Felicia does a good job of keeping us entertained."

Ginger sipped her drink and nodded. "I quite agree."

"When will you see Louisa again?"

"I've invited her to come and visit once she's finished her education."

Haley plopped the cracker into her mouth.

"Oh, there's the princess," Ginger said, peering over Haley's shoulder. "Pretend to be looking at the barman."

Haley swivelled her head slowly, covering her mouthful with one hand as nonchalantly as possible, and watched the princess stroll to a table, already occupied by a gentleman. Ginger had seen him arrive, but his hat had hidden his face, and he'd turned his back to her when he'd taken it off. All she could see was the top of his head, washed-out blond hair with noticeable streaks of grey, slicked back with hair grease and a fine-tooth comb.

"I wish I could see who she's with," Ginger said.

"You could visit the ladies," Haley said. "It'll take you right by."

"She'd recognise me." Ginger patted the bottom of her red bob. "But you could do it."

"How would I know who the man is? I don't know anyone who isn't in medicine."

"You can describe him to me. Maybe he was at the gala."

"Okay." Haley stood, straightened her dress and stepped away.

"Haley," Ginger called. "Don't forget your handbag."

"Right." Haley picked up the small clutch and moved it up to her face as she passed the princess' table.

Good move, Ginger thought. The princess might recognise Haley from the gala, even if she'd never spoken to her.

Ginger avoided eye contact with the table hosting the two gentlemen so as not to give them encouragement. Haley returned shortly and reclaimed her chair.

"So?"

"I do recognise him. He was at the gala."

Ginger leaned in closer. "Pray tell, who is it?"

141

Haley looked as if she were biting her cheek to keep from smiling. "Lord Whitmore."

Ginger's jaw slackened. "Goodness."

"*And*, they were holding hands under the table."

"No! He's having an affair?"

"From the way they looked at each other, I'd say that's a resounding yes."

"But, he's with—"

"With what?" Haley asked.

The British secret service.

"With Lady Whitmore, of course," Ginger replied. "Poor lady."

CHAPTER EIGHTEEN

*G*inger patted Haley's gloved hand. "Keep watch. I'm going to have a look at the princess' room whilst she's occupied."

"How are you going to do that? I'm sure it's locked."

Ginger cocked her head and smiled crookedly. "Have you forgotten the SS *Rosa* already?"

"Ha!" Haley said. "How could I forget that?"

"Then you remember a certain unconventional use of my hatpins," Ginger said tapping a pin that was keeping her white satin cloche from shifting.

Haley sniggered. "I do. Off with you, then."

Luckily, a shift change was in process, and a younger lift attendant had arrived to relieve the older one. This would definitely work to Ginger's advantage, as the day attendant wouldn't know that the princess had left her floor. Ginger stepped into the lift, the ornate brass doors closing her in with the young attendant. He had ruddy cheeks and fine stubble on his face. Ginger smiled brightly, lowered her chin and fluttered her mascara-heavy lashes.

"Hello, handsome," she said with her American accent. She made a show of playing with the beads that ran around her bare neck.

The rosy colour of the youth's cheeks deepened. "Madam. What floor?"

"It's Mrs. Ford."

Ginger patted the young man's arm, and his eyes widened at the familiarity.

"Have we met before?" Ginger asked. "I've only been to London a couple times, just in from the States, you know. With my husband, Henry."

The attendant gulped. "Henry Ford? The motorcar maker."

Ginger giggled. "The one and only! We've just purchased a home in Westminster."

"Welcome to London, madam!"

"Thank you."

The attendant seemed to realize that he hadn't been doing his job. "Which floor would you like, madam?

"Well, you know, I'm not sure anymore. I'm here to visit my dear friend Princess Sophia von Altenhofen." Ginger dragged her fingers through her handbag. "But I seemed to have misplaced the room number."

"It's quite all right, Mrs. Ford. She's on the top floor, number four."

"Fantastic!"

The lift shuddered upwards. Ginger tipped the lad generously and hoped that would seal his discretion. She waited until the lift lowered and the top of the attendant's head disappeared, then hurried to room four.

Ginger removed her hatpin and carefully worked the lock, easing the pins in the mechanisms as they popped one after the other. A sense of gratification filled her when she heard the slight click. She slipped inside the princess's grand room.

Ginger took a moment to admire the decor. The room was bright with pale walls and a light colour printed carpet. The bed was the largest Ginger had ever seen with a padded peach-coloured headboard and matching valance and footstool. Adjacent to the bed was a fireplace with a cement hearth painted gold. There was a white dressing table with a matching chest of drawers and an armchair with a calming peach-and-white print. A white table and chair sat in front of a large window, so huge it almost took up the whole wall.

Ginger immediately checked the dressing table, the chest of drawers, the wardrobe and the bedside tables. Coming up empty, she felt defeated. Frustrated, she scanned the room, and, on impulse she stuck a hand under the mattress. She ran her fingers along one side, across the foot of the bed, and up the opposite side. Halfway to the pillow her hand hit a bump. Removing a small black velvet sack, she opened it and peered inside.

Reverting to her American accent, she muttered, "Well, I'll be darned."

Inside was the *Blue Desire* on its sleek silver chain. She lifted it to the light. It looked real enough, but she would need a jeweller to confirm it.

Ginger dropped the blue diamond back into the bag

and slipped it between the mattress and the base where she'd found it. Her heart raced. She'd been in the room too long. The princess could return at any moment. A quick glance around the room assured Ginger that everything was left as she'd found it. She cracked the door to ensure the corridor was empty, but ducked back inside at the sound of voices, male and female.

Was it the princess and Lord Whitmore? Ginger considered where she might hide. In the wardrobe? No, the princess could easily want to change her clothes. Under the bed. She loathed the thought.

Instead of growing louder, the voices grew softer until they were muffled after the sound of a room door closing followed them.

Ginger let out a breath and rechecked the corridor. Empty. She quickly slipped out and turned the opposite direction from the lift towards the stairwell. She couldn't risk running into the princess should she decide to return to her room. She slowed when a laundry worker turned a corner. He was slight and of Indian descent. He politely averted his eyes when he passed.

She hurried down the plush carpeting of the stairwell —all four floors—until she reached the lobby. She stopped to catch her breath. Her timing was impeccable. The princess was just entering the lift and Ginger could see the young attendant's look of confusion. Hopefully he would hold his tongue. Surely Ginger's tip was still burning in the lad's pocket.

Haley entered the lobby from the lounge doors.

"There you are!"

Her friend's worry was evident in her dark eyes.

"I'm okay, Haley." Ginger reverted to her natural London accent. "I saw Princess Sophia enter the lift."

Haley's fingers went to her throat. "It scared the dickens out of me. I thought she might catch you in the act. Thank goodness you left when you did."

"It was serendipitous."

"Well? Did you find anything?"

Ginger relayed her findings.

"That blue diamond again," Haley mused.

"How did *she* get it" Ginger said. "Could she be the murderer?"

Haley lifted a shoulder. "We don't even know if it's real."

They approached the front desk.

"Excuse me," Ginger said softly, in her most feminine voice.

The male clerk looked up. "Can I help you?"

"I need to make an urgent telephone call."

The clerk produced a modern telephone, and Ginger dialled Scotland Yard requesting to speak to Chief Inspector Reed.

He wasn't too happy to hear about her unauthorised sleuthing.

"Ginger," he admonished. "What if she'd found you snooping in her room?"

"She didn't, and that's what matters. I left everything as I found it, even the blue diamond."

"I'm surprised to hear about the jewel, as Lord Lyon returned the paste to the Yard. Lady Lyon confessed to the necklace, but insisted the grand duchess was already dead."

Lady Lyon—what gumption!

"Then this must be the real one," Ginger said.

"And the killer knew this. Otherwise he or she would've taken it instead of leaving it for Lady Lyon to find."

"The princess must be our killer."

"Where is she now?"

"She went up in the lift about ten minutes ago."

"I'll get a warrant and come as soon as I can."

"We'll wait for you."

Ginger and Haley returned to the lounge where the music and chatter would keep their conversation from being overheard. They ordered brandy and spoke quietly over the flame of the candle that flickered in the centre of the table.

"Do you think Sophia von Altenhofen killed Mary Parker to steal the real *Blue Desire*?" Haley asked. "Replacing it with a fake one in hopes of avoiding detection?

"Perhaps," Ginger said after a sip. "Princess von Altenhofen admitted to knowing that the grand duchess' necklace was fake when the chief inspector and I interviewed her."

Haley pushed a curl behind her ear. "Maybe she could be so confident because she knew the real one was already in her possession."

"But why would the princess reveal her knowledge of the paste if she was the killer?" Ginger said. "She must be aware that her admittance to this fact implicates her."

"Perhaps she became *too* confident," Haley responded. "Either way, it's obvious that the princess isn't the owner of the *Blue Desire*, or she would've put up a fuss at the gala when the grand duchess arrived."

Haley clinked the ice in her glass as she peered at the amber liquid thoughtfully. "If neither the princess nor the grand duchess was the necklace's owner, who was?"

Before Ginger could surmise an answer, Basil appeared at their table. He opened his jacket and removed a folded piece of paper.

"The warrant."

"That was fast," Ginger said.

"Judge Snelling is eager to close this case. Would you join me? Since you know the whereabouts of," he paused and lowered his voice, "what we're looking for."

Ginger was already standing. "Of course. You don't mind if Miss Higgins joins us?"

Basil hesitated, then relented. "Miss Higgins."

The three of them, plus a member of housekeeping who Basil had commandeered, headed up in the lift. This time Ginger didn't greet the attendant with her American persona. Instead, Basil flashed his badge. "Police business. Top floor."

The attendant frowned, his expression serious. "Yes, sir."

Basil knocked on the princess' door. "Princess von Altenhofen? It's the police. Please open the door."

No sound came from the other side and Basil knocked again. When the door remained unopened, he motioned to the chambermaid to unlock the door.

"Oh, mercy," Ginger whispered.

Princess Sophia von Altenhofen lay on the bed, skin pale as porcelain, her lifeless eyes wide open.

CHAPTER NINETEEN

*H*aley immediately checked for a pulse, both at the neck and the wrists. She glanced at Ginger and Basil and shook her head. "She's dead but warm. This happened very recently."

Basil dashed out into the hall, searched both directions, and whisked back into the room. "I'll go to the front desk and call the station. Are you all right to stay here?"

"Of course," Ginger said. "I doubt whoever did this will return."

Basil nodded, reassured, and disappeared.

Haley carefully examined the body.

"Can you determine the cause of death?"

"It appears to be a broken neck."

"Similar to Mary Parker?"

"Seems so."

Ginger moved to the opposite side of the bed and reached under the mattress. She frowned and swept her arm back and forth.

"What's wrong?" Haley asked.

"The *Blue Desire*," Ginger said. "It's gone."

"Maybe the killer came for what he or she had intended to steal last time."

"Except that Lady Lyon admitted to taking the fake after Mary Parker was killed." Ginger began to search the dressing table drawers.

"Unless she's lying," Haley said from her position on the bed.

Ginger considered her. "You think Lady Lyon did this?"

"I don't think you can rule it out just yet."

"She didn't have any scratches on her arms."

Haley lifted her chin. "There's that, I suppose."

"And what about the cigarette paper code?" Ginger said. "How does that fit in?"

"I don't know. But whoever did this was at the Ritz at the same time we were."

"When you walked across the room, did you notice anyone besides Lord Whitmore who was at the gala?"

Haley shook her head. "Why? Do you think Lord Whitmore did this? He could've gone up the stairs quickly while the princess took the elevator."

"But I'd just come down the stairs. I would've seen him in the lobby."

"Unless he saw you first and ducked behind a plant or into the men's room."

Ginger huffed. "Such a mystery."

Basil returned, and Ginger broke the news of the missing diamond and the conclusions, or lack thereof, she and Haley had come to.

Shortly afterward, Sergeant Scott and two constables arrived. Basil filled Ginger and Haley in.

"There's no sign of forced entry," he said.

"No apparent defensive wounds," Haley added, "though the princess is wearing elbow-length gloves. Bruises may be visible in the post-mortem."

"So it was likely she knew her attacker," Ginger said.

Basil scribbled in his notepad. "It would appear so."

A constable tapped on the door. "Sir, the medical examiner is here."

Ginger expected Dr. Watts to enter the room and held in her surprise when the handsome Dr. Gupta walked in.

"Chief Inspector," Dr. Gupta said, then acknowledged the ladies with a quick nod of the head before attending to the body. Within minutes he came to the same conclusion Haley had. "Broken neck. Bruising heavier on one side."

"The left?" Ginger asked.

"Possibly. It depends if the attacker approached from the front or back. I'll know more after the post-mortem. Estimated time of death to be one hour ago based on body temperature and the pooling of blood."

Another tap on the door. "Sir, the ambulance has arrived."

Two men entered with a stretcher and gently lifted the princess' body onto it.

Dr. Gupta signed the papers authorising moving the body to the city mortuary. He turned to Haley. "Miss Higgins, would you like to assist me?"

"I would," she said, already removing the beads from

her neck. She handed them to Ginger. "I'll take a taxicab home."

Ginger could feel Basil's eyes on her as she watched Haley leave with Dr. Gupta. She folded her arms as she turned to him.

"I had a visit from Superintendent Morris today."

"Oh. I take it that it didn't go well?"

"No, it did not. He all but accused me of killing Mary Parker."

"I'm sorry."

"Did you know?"

"I knew he fancied that theory," Basil said. "I tried to talk him out of it, but the man can be a bulldog with a bone when he wants to. I've learned to let him race ahead until he hits a brick wall." His eyes softened. "I regret that you had to suffer through that."

Ginger blew out her frustration. Basil couldn't be held accountable for the actions of his boss, and at least he had tried.

She changed the subject. "Did you happen to spot Lord Whitmore at any point this evening?"

"No. Why would I?"

"Because he was in the lounge earlier with Princess Sophia. They were, you could say, getting cosy."

Basil blinked. "An affair?"

"It looked that way."

"He was at the gala, too," Basil said, considering. "Perhaps his amorous activities extended beyond the princess. He kills them when he's finished with them."

Ginger opened a dressing table drawer and fished through the princess' underthings. Earlier she'd searched these drawers in a rush. It was possible she'd missed something. "I can't believe that."

Taking Ginger's cue, Basil opened the wardrobe and examined the contents. "Why not?"

Ginger stilled and turned to him. "I don't know if you're aware, Basil, but Lord Whitmore works for MI5."

Basil swivelled on his heel to face her. His jaw dropped as his eyes narrowed, drilling into hers. "How do you know this?"

"I can't really say, only that was what I heard during the war. I thought he might've retired by now, but perhaps not," Ginger said.

Basil stepped towards her. "Do you think Lord Whitmore killed Mary Parker as part of an assignment?"

"If she was passing on information he—or should I say, 'the crown'—didn't want to get out, then yes, it's possible. And if that's the case, you'll never get a conviction. Especially if she was working for both the Russians and the British."

Basil rubbed the back of his neck. "And I suppose that would be true of the princess, should Lord Whitmore be the culprit here as well."

"I'm afraid so."

"Blast it."

Ginger closed the top drawer and opened the second. "Was the princess part of the mission with the grand duchess or just unlucky?"

"Good question," Basil said. "Who would know such a thing?"

Ginger wrinkled her nose as the answer came to her. "Captain Francis Smithwick."

Basil groaned, sharing Ginger's dislike of the man. They'd both met Captain Smithwick during the war. Ginger had worked under his command and found his methods to be, at best, distasteful and at worst unscrupulous. Wanting Ginger to join his team again, he had manoeuvred his way into her life while she'd been visiting Ambrosia and Felicia the previous autumn at their home in Hertfordshire, Bray Manor. Of course, she'd refused. He'd stooped so low as to play with Felicia's emotions just to get Ginger's attention, which was simply unforgivable.

"I'll see if I can track him down," Basil said. "In the meantime, I think we need to visitLord and Lady Whitmore again."

CHAPTER TWENTY

Ginger insisted on driving her own motorcar and meeting Basil at the Whitmore manor. She told him it would be more convenient afterwards when it was time to go home, when the truth was she just wasn't ready to be in confined quarters with him again. She'd made the mistake of leaving her heart unguarded, and try as she might it had been impossible for her to revert emotionally to their earlier colleague-only status. It didn't help that he smelled good.

Arriving ahead of Ginger, Basil was waiting for her to drive up. He opened her door and assisted her out of the Daimler. the chief inspector's polite manner was one of the qualities that had attracted Ginger to him, but now she wished he'd been a little more of a cad.

Once at the manor entrance, the wooden door was opened by a bland-faced butler.

"I'm Chief Inspector Reed and this is Lady Gold. AreLord and Lady Whitmore in?"

"Indeed. Do come inside." The butler closed the door

against the cold evening breeze. The spicy warmth of a nearby fireplace enveloped Ginger.

"Lady Whitmore is in the sitting room, and Lord Whitmore is in his study."

"We'd be pleased to see Lady Whitmore alone," Basil said. "Later you can show us to Lord Whitmore's study."

The butler led them through the entrance hall to the sitting room, the door of which stood ajar. "Chief Inspector Reed and Lady Gold, madam."

The butler backed out and closed the door.

Lady Whitmore's mouth fell open. She took a moment to gather her wits before standing in welcome.

"This is a surprise."

"I have some enquiries, madam," Basil said.

"I assumed. It's quite late to be making uninvited social calls. Please have a seat."

Lady Whitmore returned to her easy chair which was angled toward the hearth while Ginger and Basil claimed seats on either side of a plush pincushion chesterfield.

Lady Whitmore clasped her hands on her lap. "So how can I help?"

"Lady Whitmore," Ginger began. "What were you looking for on the upper floor of my shop?"

Lady Whitmore blinked in surprise. "I'd assumed you were after information about . . . someone else."

"Who else?" Basil asked.

"Well, I don't know. That's what most of my visitors want."

"Gossip?" Ginger said.

"I prefer the term *counsel*."

If Lady Whitmore thought she'd distracted Ginger

from the original question, she was mistaken. "What did you expect to find in my shop, Lady Whitmore?"

Lady Whitmore worked her hands together as her eyes scanned the ceiling. "I suspect you already know, since you're here asking about it."

"I'd like you to tell me, regardless."

Lady Whitmore stared at Ginger like a trapped animal. "It was an article of clothing. I will say no more."

"Did Lord Whitmore ask you to run the errand?" Basil asked.

"I really cannot say."

Basil stood. "Thank you for your time, Lady Whitmore."

The matron's eyes darted from Basil to Ginger and to her hands. Ginger thought she must believe she'd got off rather easily. Surely, she had to realise she'd answered the questions by how she *didn't* answer them.

"I'm always happy to help."

"In that case," Basil said, "can you please direct us to Lord Whitmore's study?"

Lady Whitmore grew pale at the request. "Why do you need to see him?"

"Just general enquiries, madam."

Lady Whitmore called for the butler. "Milroy, please let Lord Whitmore know he has guests."

Lady Whitmore spun on her heels and with head bowed returned to the sitting room. Ginger couldn't help but wonder what Lady Whitmore knew about her husband, but it was evident by the lady's discomfort she probably knew too much.

Lord Whitmore didn't hide his displeasure at being

interrupted. He was well on his way through a tumbler of whisky and Ginger guessed it wasn't his first.

"Well, come in and sit down, then," he said. "Can I get you a drink?"

"No, thank you," Basil said. Ginger knew the chief inspector didn't like to drink while investigating. Keeping a clear head was important. Sometimes, it could be a matter of life and death.

"I doubt you're here for pleasantries," Lord Whitmore grumbled, "so get on with it."

"What can you tell us about Mary Parker?"

"Not much."

"When did you become aware that the grand duchess wasn't really a grand duchess?"

The man shrugged. "Most likely when everyone else did. I read the papers."

Ginger hadn't expected the man to be forthcoming. She wondered if Basil would bring up the cigarette paper, but then again, they were there to solve a murder—two murders—not solve a diplomatic problem.

"What do you know about a blue diamond necklace called the *Blue Desire*?" Basil asked.

Lord Whitmore set his glass on his desk with more strength than necessary. "I demand to know what this is all about. Not only is this impertinent, but it's also a waste of my time."

"Were you having an affair, Lord Whitmore?" Ginger asked. "With Princess Sophia von Altenhofen?"

Lord Whitmore jumped to his feet. "That is enough. I must ask you to leave!"

Basil remained unruffled by the big man's outburst.

"Lord Whitmore," Basil said calmly. "Did you kill the princess?"

Lord Whitmore's bluster evaporated as he slowly sank into his chair. "What are you saying?"

"Princess Sophia von Altenhofen was murdered tonight."

Ginger watched Lord Whitmore's expression. She knew he was trained to control his emotions, to play whatever part was necessary, but he was still human. The pink hue of his ruddy skin deepened. The war had been over for five years, long enough to get out of practice. Ginger knew this from experience.

"Dear God." The man's face went ashen and he downed the rest of his whisky.

"When did you last see the princess?" Basil asked.

"Earlier tonight at the Ritz lounge, as you must well know," Lord Whitmore replied. "Why else would you be here asking questions?"

Basil conceded with a nod. "What time did you last see her?"

"I left at nine o'clock."

Basil glanced at Ginger and she gave a subtle nod. That was the time Ginger had left the top floor, and the princess had stepped into the lift.

Lord Whitmore continued, "I can assure you that the princess was very much alive when I left. I saw her get into the lift."

"Were you having an affair with the princess, Lord Whitmore, or were you just making a play?" Ginger asked. She gave him a knowing look.

Lord Whitmore leaned back in his chair with a sigh. "It

was an affair. Early days. We hadn't even . . . Please, there's no reason for my wife to know."

"We promise to reveal only what is necessary to solve the murders," Basil said, standing. "We'll contact you when we have more questions.

Ginger turned back for one last question. "Lord Whitmore, had the princess been engaged by MI5?"

Lord Whitmore slowly shook his head. "No. We met at your gala, Lady Gold." He pointed towards the door. "Milroy will show you out."

As they left, he poured himself another drink.

CHAPTER TWENTY-ONE

To Ginger's surprise, the next morning, the Romanian Countess, Andreea Balcescu, entered Feathers & Flair. She wore a floor-length, fur-trimmed Etruscan red wool coat and a powder-blue woollen scarf.

"Good morning, Countess!" Ginger said. "You can't imagine how happy I am to see you. I'd been told you had disappeared into thin air."

The countess smacked her ruby red lips. "You English are so dramatic. I have been at Brown's Hotel the whole time. I simply register under another name."

"Why is that?"

The countess clicked her tongue. "Clearly you have not been to the east lately."

"Yes, I suppose one can't be too careful. Is there something here I can help you find?"

"I would rather look around on my own, if you do not mind."

"Certainly. Please let me or Madame Roux know if you'd like help with anything."

Ginger busied herself at the counter, pretending not to be watching the countess, even though that was exactly what she was doing. New customers entered, creating a bit of a diversion. Ginger sent Madame Roux to greet them. Out of the corner of her eye, Ginger saw Countess Balcescu cast a quick glance over her shoulder before heading upstairs.

Ginger smirked. Even the royals were interested in what the factories produced. Madame Roux returned to the cash counter and asked Ginger if the mannequins in the windows were due to have their outfits swapped over. Ginger nodded and gave instructions, losing track of time. How long had Countess Balcescu been upstairs? Was Dorothy helping her to try things on?

No, Dorothy had just come through the velvet curtain from the back. Ginger decided to venture upstairs herself when the countess appeared.

"Countess Balcescu," Ginger said. "Can I offer assistance?"

The countess hesitated. "This is going to sound silly, but I believe I dropped something upstairs, on the night of the gala. I confess to being curious and took a look around. I only wanted to see if it was still there."

"What is it that you lost? I'll ask the girls if they found anything."

"It is all right. It is not there. I must be mistaken as to where I dropped it. Good day, Lady Gold." The countess hurried to the exit.

Ginger called after her, "What did you drop?" Could

the countess be looking for the shawl and its hidden message as well?

Countess Balcescu was out of the front door before she could reply. She was in such a hurry to leave, she didn't notice that her powder-blue wool scarf had fallen to the floor. Ginger scooped it up. A faint smell of after-shave emanated from the fabric, barely noticeable under the heavy perfume the countess fancied. Ginger had a fleeting thought that perhaps Princess Sophia hadn't been Lord Whitmore's only conquest.

There was something frightfully strange about Countess Balcescu. Without taking time to grab her coat Ginger followed the lady outside. The countess proved to be quick on her feet, and Ginger just barely caught the flash of the red wool of the countess's coat as she disappeared around the corner.

Trotting after the lady, Ginger quickly realised that her shoes were not fit for the wet weather, and she almost slipped on the pavement. Her poor frock was becoming utterly ruined along with her hair, but she pushed into the rain anyway, turning the same corner the countess had.

Ginger's eyes scanned the area but a pinkish-red coat could not be found. The entrance to the Piccadilly Circus Station was nearby and Ginger, crossing her arms over chest and curling against the rain, hurried around the bend and followed the throng of weather-weary citizens underground. It was a great relief to be out of the wet, but the wind that billowed through the tunnel was chilly.

In a very unladylike fashion, Ginger slipped on the stairs. The railing saved her dignity, but not her stockings. She felt the rip ladder its way up her thigh.

When she arrived at the platform, a red coat slid into the carriage just as the doors were closing and the train pulled away.

Ginger missed catching the countess, but she was fairly certain she might just catch a cold! By the time she got back to the shop she was a sopping mess.

"*Mon Dieu*!" Madame Roux said, when Ginger burst through the doors. "What on earth has got into you?"

Ginger struggled to come up with an explanation. "I thought I saw someone through the windows…"

"Stay there," Madame Roux instructed. "I don't want you dripping on the floors." She disappeared behind the curtain to the back and returned within seconds with Ginger's coat in hand. "You must go home before you catch pneumonia!"

Ginger quickly put the woollen coat on and wrapped it tightly around her chest, relishing in its warmth. What she needed now was a change of clothes and a good hot cup of tea!

CHAPTER TWENTY-TWO

*M*adame Roux encouraged Ginger to head home *tout de suite*! and Ginger agreed. It did her business no good appearing like a drowned rat, and she had no time to nurse a cold should one latch on.

"Leave your wet hat behind and take mine," Madame Roux insisted. Ginger stopped her before she left for the back area where they kept their personal items.

"No, no, Madame Roux. Then what will you wear? Besides, I have a wall full of hats to choose from," Ginger said pointing to the display in her store. "Please bring me the blue wool cloche."

Madame Roux did as instructed and Ginger pulled it down on her head. "Thank you, Madam Roux. Do remember to mark it down in the books that I owe for this."

"I shall, now off you go," Madame Roux was eager to get Ginger out of the shop and Ginger didn't blame her.

The Daimler was parked across the street, it was as close to Feathers & Flair as possible, but unless she was up to running across traffic she had to walk around to where the traffic policeman was directing irate drivers. Sleet had begun to fall, though that didn't slow drivers down. It seemed that everyone was in a hurry. How quickly one forgot what transportation by horse and carriage was like after travelling fifteen miles an hour through the city in a motorcar for a few months. One even stopped noticing that horse-drawn carriages still shared the road.

Ginger sat up in her motorcar, cursing its complicated procedure, and again promising herself she'd get a new motorcar one day. She set the ignition, the throttle, and then the choke before reaching for the starter button with her foot. She put her weight on the button, and the engine sputtered to life.

Pressing the clutch to the floor, she put the motorcar into first gear then, while slowly releasing the clutch with one foot, she added petrol with the other. The motorcar didn't have a heater, but simply starting the beast was enough to work up a sweat.

Unlike Boston, where snow, and lots of it, was a natural part of winter, Londoners had little practice driving in winter conditions. If it snowed it wasn't very heavy and didn't last long. Mostly, it was endless dreary days of rain. Ginger had forgotten after so many winter seasons away, but it all came back to her now.

Ginger signalled to cut into the crowded mass of vehicles that inched their way towards Mayfair. One really ought to draw lines on the road and make clear lanes, Ginger thought. Someone was going to get in an—

The motorcar in front of her suddenly stopped and even though Ginger pumped the brake, it wasn't enough to keep her from slipping along the sleet buildup and slamming into the vehicle's back bumper. Her body jerked backwards just as the Daimler was hit from behind. Horns blared loudly.

Ginger clasped the back of her neck and yelped. "Oh, my word!"

She tried to open the driver's door, but the latch wouldn't give. She was stuck! A man rushed to the passenger side, swung that door open, and stretched out his hand.

"Madam, let me help you."

"I don't know if I can move around the gear stick." She groaned. "I've done something to my neck."

"Just go slowly, madam. I'm parked on the next street out of 'arms way. I can take you to the surgery."

Ginger did as she was urged. She eased across the front bench seat, untangling her coat as she passed the gear stick.

"This is so kind of you, Mr . . . "

"Ward."

"Mr. Ward."

The man tipped his flat cap. "If it were my wife, I'd 'ope someone would 'elp 'er in a pinch like this."

A police officer approached. "Madam, is this your motorcar?"

Ginger stared at the damaged Daimler, both bumpers crushed and the headlamps broken.

"It is. Is it all right for me to leave it here?"

"We'll have it towed away, madam. Can I have your name and telephone number, if you have one?"

"Lady Gold. Mallowan 1355."

The officer scribbled the information on his notepad. "Did you see what happened?"

Mr. Ward interjected. "Officer, the lady's trembling."

Ginger hadn't noticed how badly she was shaking until the gentleman mentioned it.

"Yes, very well. Someone will call you, Lady Gold."

As Mr. Ward ushered Ginger away, she cradled her wounded neck.

"Please would you bring my handbag, Mr. Ward?"

The kindly man darted back to the Daimler, found the bag in question on the floor, and carried it for Ginger. She memorised Mr. Ward's vehicle registration number and would ask Pippins to send him a token of thanks.

Ginger wasn't the only driver from the pileup to be taken to the nearest surgery, which belonged to Dr. Warren Longden, the doctor she'd met before on a previous case when a death had occurred in the drawing room at Hartigan House. On that occasion a lord appeared to have succumbed to a heart attack but it turned out to be something far more sinister.

A nurse accompanied Ginger to one of the patient rooms, asked Ginger preliminary questions, and made notes in her file.

While Ginger waited her turn to see the doctor, she mentally reviewed the case. The blue diamond worn by Mary Parker in her role as a Russian grand duchess was a paste. Miss Parker delivered her shawl with its secret message to the upper floor at Feathers & Flair, too early for the intended recipient to have the opportunity to pick it up. Lady Lyon stole the fake diamond, but insisted that Miss Parker was already dead.

Princess Sophia von Altenhofen knew the diamond Miss Parker wore to the gala was fake because the real one was under a mattress in her suite at the Ritz. Lord Whitmore, a British agent, was careful not to incriminate himself in the death of Miss Parker. He gave no information about what she had hidden in the shawl, or about the code written on the cigarette paper. He'd sent his wife on an errand to retrieve the shawl, but she'd failed.

Lord Whitmore admitted to having an affair with the princess. Whether or not the princess had been involved in any espionage was unclear.

A tap on the door announced Dr. Longden.

"Lady Gold," he said kindly. "I hear you've got caught up in a motorcar accident."

"Yes. With the sleet coming on, the road became slippery."

"A four-car pileup," Dr. Longden said. He moved the eyeglasses that rested on the top of his grey head onto his nose and referred to his notes. "Apparently you were the third vehicle."

"How do you know?"

"I just treated the gentleman who was in front of you."

Ginger groaned. She supposed all the vehicles involved were now on their way to a motorcar garage for repairs.

The doctor dug through the pocket of his white coat and flashed a small but bright torch into her eyes. "Where does it hurt?"

"The back of my neck, all the way up to my skull."

"Yes. I fear you have pulled the muscles in your neck."

"I see," Ginger said. "How do you treat it?"

"Aspirin for the pain. Rest, of course. But it's imperative that you don't injure your neck further. Thankfully, the impact was at low speed. I'll outfit you with a neck brace to speed up the healing process."

Oh, mercy.

"Perhaps you should lie down while you wait."

A wave of fatigue washed over her with the suggestion. She almost nodded in agreement, but caught herself before she moved her head. "Yes."

Dr. Longden helped swing her legs up on the examination table and lowered her slowly until her head rested on a pillow.

Her eyes immediately fluttered close.

A tapping on the door followed. The nurse entered. "Lady Gold, you have someone here who insists on seeing you. Seeing as he's your vicar, I've allowed it."

Ginger smiled at the sight of Oliver Hill's lanky body and crooked grin. His ginger brows lifted at seeing her.

"Ginger, I came as soon as I heard."

"How *did* you hear?"

"One of my parishioners witnessed the motorcar smash. He recognised you."

"Darn red hair."

Oliver smiled. "You are going to be all right, aren't you?"

"Of course, I am. I'm just waiting for a special piece of jewellery to arrive, and then the good doctor shall allow me to go home."

Oliver scratched his head. "Jewellery?"

"A neck brace."

"Ah, of course."

"It was good of you to come, Oliver. I admit, the whole thing gave me a fright. At first, I thought I may have broken my neck. I was never so glad to be able to wiggle my fingers and toes, especially since they were already frozen stiff."

Oliver placed his hand on her arm in a gesture of comfort. "I'm always here for you, Ginger."

Another tap on the door and instead of Dr. Longden, the nurse entered again. "You're a popular lady, Lady Gold. If he weren't the Chief Inspector…"

"Basil?"

"I don't mean to intrude," Basil said as he removed his hat. "I heard about the accident and when your name appeared on the list of drivers involved . . . I wanted to make sure you were okay."

"Like I was telling Reverend Hill," Ginger said, "I'm waiting on the doctor for a neck brace, and then I can rest at home."

Oliver stood and moved away from the examination table. The room was small, and the two men juggled to find a spot to stand whilst keeping a comfortable distance between them.

Oliver reached out his hand. "Hello, Chief Inspector. I don't believe we've met. I'm Oliver Hill, vicar at St. George's City of London."

They shook hands while Basil said, "How do you do, Reverend?"

Basil looked to Ginger and back to Oliver. "And how do you two know each other?"

"Ginger . . . Lady Gold, very generously set up a

charity through our diocese to help feed the children who live in the streets."

Basil ducked his chin. "Lady Gold is indeed generous."

Ginger felt self-conscious. "Reverend Hill does the majority of the work."

"Well, with the help of my secretary, Mrs. Davies. She's very good at organizing things."

Basil drummed his hat with his fingers. "Splendid."

An awkward silence descended.

Ginger couldn't help comparing the two men as they stood side by side. Attractive in a conventional way, Basil stood straight with dark hair and brooding hazel eyes. His well-fitted suit and tie, polished leather shoes, and new hat completed the look. He was the law, and there was no denying the authority he possessed.

Oliver was taller and more slender, with a tendency to hunch to lessen his height. His blue-green eyes were trimmed with pale lashes. Freckles were sprinkled across his nose. Wayward wavy red hair sprang out in various directions in spite of the weight of the oil he used to manage it. Though not model handsome, he had a very pleasing face, always smiled, and possessed a childlike joy. His standard wear of the black vicar's robe and white collar gave him a commanding presence, although his was of the spiritual kind.

Dr. Longden's return to the room snapped Ginger out of her thoughts. He stared in surprise at the two men. "Hello, Chief Inspector Reed, Reverend Hill."

Along with Ginger, the doctor had worked with Basil on the case that transpired in the drawing room of

Hartigan House, but how were the doctor and Oliver acquainted?

Oliver answered her unspoken question.

"We've missed you at St. George's, Doctor."

"Yes, well, I've been busy with my practice. Perhaps this Sunday." He squeezed inside holding the neck brace up in the air. "Um, if you gentlemen wouldn't mind?"

"I'll wait for you, Ginger," Basil said. "I'd be happy to drive you home."

"No, no," Oliver countered. "It would be my pleasure to give you a lift, Ginger."

"He's right, Basil," Ginger said. "You have other ... *responsibilities*." The frustrated look on Basil's face pleased her. After all, there *was* Emelia Reed to consider.

"Very well. Good day." Basil said, begrudgingly. He placed his trilby on his head, gave a quick nod, and turned on his heel.

As if he'd just won a round, Oliver beamed.

And who knew? Ginger thought. Maybe he had.

CHAPTER TWENTY-THREE

Ginger couldn't escape the notice of Pippins' ever-watchful eye. It didn't help that she hadn't arrived by the back entrance like she usually did when driving the Daimler. Instead, she came through the front entrance assisted by the reverend.

A look of horror crossed the butler's wrinkled face when he took in the neck brace. "Good gracious, madam!"

"Your mistress has been in a motorcar smash," Oliver explained.

Pippins hurried to Ginger's side. "Are you all right?"

"Nothing that a hot bath and a cup of tea won't cure."

"I'll send Lizzie upstairs straightaway to draw you a bath. Where would you like to go right now? The sitting room or upstairs?"

"I believe I'll go straight to my room." Ginger longed to finally peel off her wet things.

"I'll assist Lady Gold upstairs," Oliver said. Pippins bowed, then went to search for Lizzie.

"Place your arm in mine for balance," Oliver instructed.

Ginger acquiesced and took hold of the banister with one hand and Oliver's arm with the other. Unfortunately, they ran into Ambrosia who was on her way down.

"Oh, dear Lord, Georgia! What on earth?"

"It's nothing, Grandmother. I only got caught in a little motorcar incident."

"I knew an accident with that thing was inevitable. Everyone has to have an automobile these days. No wonder there's not enough room on the road for everyone." She shook her head in disapproval, the soft skin on her face jiggling with the effort.

"The sleet was the culprit, Grandmother."

"But you've been injured!"

"Just a pulled muscle. I'll be okay in no time."

Ambrosia narrowed her gaze at Oliver. "Since you're a man of the cloth, I allow for you to help Lady Gold to her room, but not an inch over the threshold!"

"Yes, milady," Oliver said seriously. "I wouldn't think of it."

Ambrosia continued on, one bony hand gripping the banister and the other on her silver-handled walking stick.

Ginger paused at her bedroom door. "I can make it from here," she said. "Since you're officially my friend now, it's my duty to save you from my grandmother-in-law's wrath."

Oliver smiled and bowed. "It's been my pleasure to take you this far."

Ginger rested her hand on the doorknob. "Well, thank

you."

"May I ask, and please don't think me presumptuous or uncaring," the reverend averted his eyes and then looked directly at Ginger. "Will you still be attending the dance?"

"Dance? Oh, yes, the charity event." Ginger had been so distracted the last few days that she'd completely forgotten about it.

"When is it, again?"

"Saturday night." Oliver gestured to his neck. "I can understand with your . . ."

Ginger placed her fingers along her neck brace. The aspirin Dr. Longden had given her had worked, and her neck didn't feel nearly as sore as it had earlier. The weekend was four days away.

"I think I should be all right to attend, Oliver, but I don't think I'll be doing any dancing."

"I'll pick you up since you no longer have a motorcar. It'll be good for the people to see your dedication. Oh, I do hope that doesn't sound unfeeling. Your health and wellbeing, of course, take top priority."

"It's okay, Oliver. I want the charity dance to be a success as much as you do."

"Great, I'll pick you up at seven."

It sounded suspiciously like a date. She'd agreed to friendship, but Ginger didn't want Oliver to believe it could ever be more than that. "Miss Gold and the dowager shall need a lift, too."

"Splendid. I'm honoured to drive all the Gold ladies. I'll pick you up at seven."

Oliver paused at the door before he left, taking in her

discomfort. "I'll find your maid."

"Thank you, Oliver." Ginger had to admire the vicar's thoughtfulness.

She eased into one of her bedroom chairs and attempted to strip out of her wet clothing. Her hosiery was particularly difficult to remove, and Ginger was tempted to get the scissors and just cut the darn things off.

She collapsed in relief when Lizzie tapped on her door.

"Bath is ready for you, madam. And Reverend Hill told me you need help undressing."

"That's correct. I do."

Lizzie expertly removed Ginger's clothing, all the time remaining professional and discreet. "The reverend is quite a handsome man, isn't he?"

Ginger stilled. "I suppose he is."

"Do you know if he's married?"

Though Ginger had no right to feel anything regarding the vicar, her maid's question annoyed her.

"It's my understanding that he's currently content without a wife."

"I see." Lizzie wrapped Ginger in a satin dressing gown and helped her to the bathroom.

Black and white tiles covered the floor. A rectangular yellow mat lay in front of the porcelain claw-foot bathtub. Ginger removed her collar and handed it to Lizzie, then carefully lowered herself into the tub. The warmth of the streaming water felt silky. Hoping the hot water would loosen the muscles of her neck, she dipped down until the water touched her chin.

"I added some salts to the water," Lizzie said. "I've heard it's good for relaxing the body."

"Thank you, Lizzie, you're a gem. I'll ring when I'm ready to get out."

Lizzie placed the hand bell on the edge of the tub, turned off the tap, and left Ginger alone.

GINGER WAS ABOUT to ring the bell when Lizzie tapped on the bathroom door. "Madam, there's a caller for you. I told him you were indisposed, but he said it was urgent."

Ginger's mind raced through the possibilities. She couldn't imagine a caller who could possibly have an 'urgent' message other than Oliver or Basil. "Who is it?"

"A Captain Smithwick, madam."

Despite the warmth of the bathwater, Ginger's blood cooled.

"Where is he now?"

"In the sitting room."

Ginger held her breath as she recalled Felicia's plans for the day. It would be dreadful for her to accidentally run into him after how he had treated her in the past. The captain had led her sister-in-law to believe that he fancied her, in fact was preparing to ask for her hand in marriage. In the end, the blighter had admitted to Ginger that he was only using Felicia to get to her.

Ginger could relax. Felicia was auditioning with Matthew Haines at the Abbott Theatre today.

"Tell the captain I'll be with him shortly."

"Yes, madam. Please wait, and I'll help you to get ready."

Ginger's head began to throb as her neck tightened, and she reluctantly agreed she could use her maid's help. Lizzie returned before too long, and soon, Ginger was out of the tub, dry, and with the neck brace fastened around her neck.

If it hadn't been for the supposed urgency, Ginger wouldn't have worried about letting the captain wait. As it was, her curiosity was piqued. Basil had obviously made an attempt to contact the captain, and here he was in her sitting room.

"The green tea dress shall do," she said to Lizzie. "The white scarf for my neck. It won't hide this unbecoming collar, but it'll mask it a little.

Lizzie did as instructed. She decorated Ginger's face with makeup and helped her into her strappy shoes.

Ginger did a slow turn in front of the mirror. "What do you think, Boss?"

Boss's stubby tail shimmied in approval. He stretched, jumped off the bed and followed Ginger out.

"Do you need my help downstairs, madam?" Lizzie asked.

"I think I'll be fine. I do feel much better . . ." Except for a low-grade headache throbbing at the base of her neck, that was. "But I wouldn't mind taking another aspirin before going down. Would you mind fetching the ones the doctor sent home with me? They're in my dressing gown pocket."

Lizzie opened the small bottle and eased one aspirin into her palm. She handed it along with the glass of water from the bedside table to Ginger.

"Thank you," Ginger said, before she swallowed the pill.

Ginger paused just outside the sitting room doors and took a fortifying breath. She stepped forward with all the confidence she could muster.

"Captain Smithwick. What a surprise."

Tea had been served and the captain set his cup and saucer down before standing and swivelling to face her. He was a large, imposing man dressed in a blue-striped suit. It'd been a while since Ginger had seen him out of uniform. His hair was parted down the side, trimmed around the ears and greased back. Lines formed around his dark eyes as he smiled—not a smile of affection though, but of conceit.

"Hello, Ginger."

Ginger despised his use of familiarity but ignored it. Lizzie had followed her in and poured her some tea. Ginger accepted the cup once she was seated.

"That's an interesting accessory," Captain Smithwick said, nodding at Ginger's neck brace.

"Yes, well, I had a little accident with the Daimler this afternoon."

"I see."

"What brings you to London?" The last Ginger had heard, the captain had been stationed in St. Albans.

He stared at her. "Work."

Ginger sat and casually crossed her legs. She sipped her tea, not allowing him to intimidate her.

"You set your little detective on me," Smithwick said with contempt. "Whatever for?"

She pursed her lips in disgust at the captain's effort to

demean Basil, but she didn't react.

"Did you speak to him?"

"I did not."

"And why not?"

"Because, *Lady Gold*, I thought to myself, what an excellent excuse to pay my good friend a visit. For old times' sake."

The man infuriated her! And in return, her head throbbed all the more. I must take some more aspirin, Ginger thought. She calmly sipped her tea, refusing to appear bothered. She and the captain were *not* friends. Her animosity toward him went further back than the ignoble way he'd treated her sister-in-law. It went back to France. He had been her superior at the time, and she had often disagreed with his approach, so reckless and often blatant in his disregard for human life. For Francis Smithwick, only the mission mattered.

"I believe the secret service may be involved in the death of Mary Parker," Ginger said. "An agent apparently working for both the Russians and the British was killed, coincidently, in my shop."

"Oh, yes. I heard about that. A nasty inconvenience I can imagine."

"Do you know anything about that?"

Captain Smithwick leaned forward and smirked. "If I did, you know I couldn't tell you. So the answer, of course, is no."

Ginger feared as much.

"Was Princess Sophia von Altenhofen part of the mission?"

"I've no idea what you're talking about."

Ginger snorted in exasperation. "Francis, why did you come?"

"As I said . . ." He lifted his teacup. "A friendly visit. So how are you, Ginger? Besides the inconvenient neck problem. I understand the chief inspector has got back with his wife. I dare say, that must sting."

"You're despicable."

"I've been called worse."

Ginger relieved herself of her teacup and stood. "If you've nothing more substantial to offer, I bid you good day."

"Now, now, don't be so hasty. I'm not the kind to visit an old friend without bringing a gift of some sort. Please sit."

Ginger hesitated, but then did as the captain bid. She couldn't let her pride get in the way, even if the chance of Smithwick's offering something of merit was infinitesimal.

"Very well," she said. "Let's have it."

"You know I can't say much since you're no longer part of the team."

"I'm aware."

"You could change that."

"I'm not interested," she replied. Especially if it meant working under Smithwick's command again.

"Such a pity." Smithwick stood and tugged on his waistcoat. "Whoever killed Mary Parker, it wasn't one of ours."

"Are you sure?"

"Quite."

So that meant it couldn't have been Lord Whitmore.

"Are you saying MI5 isn't involved?" Ginger tried to be nonchalant.

"Sorry, but I'm afraid you'll get no more from me."

Voices erupted from the entrance hall. Felicia asked Pippins where Ginger could be found.

"Quick!" she said, moving toward the captain. "You must leave through the kitchen."

"Why? Shall I not greet Miss Gold before I go?"

"You most certainly shall not!"

Ginger was desperate to spare Felicia further upset. "Please. I appeal to your sense of decency, Captain."

"Very well. You may show me out like a common servant."

Ginger had no qualms about that. Her opinion of her servants topped that of what she held for Smithwick by a long shot. Though it pained her physically to do it, she hurried him across the sitting room practically pushing him through the dining room door.

"Lizzie!"

Thankfully the young maid was within hearing distance in the kitchen. She scampered into the dining room and stopped short in surprise at seeing Captain Smithwick standing there with a scowl on his face.

"Madam?"

"Please show the Captain out through the morning room. He's expressed interest in seeing the garden, and with my injury—"

Smithwick gave her a sharp look. As if he'd be interested in her garden and in *January*.

Lizzie bobbed, her chin down. It wasn't her place to question her mistress. "Please follow me."

Ginger leaned against the wall to catch her breath. That beastly Smithwick! Would she ever manage to rid her life of him?

"Are you all right, madam?"

Mrs. Beasley poked her head into the dining room, obviously struck with curiosity at the sight of one such as the Captain being escorted out of the back door by Lizzie. She stared at Ginger with concern.

Ginger brushed at her dress. "Yes. Of course. I just needed a bit of fresh air. I'm quite all right now."

"Are you sure? I heard about your accident."

"I'm fine. Just a sore neck."

"I'll send Grace in with some more tea in the sitting room and bring out a plate of sandwiches."

"That would be marvellous, Mrs. Beasley. I believe Felicia is home, as well."

"We'll make enough for two, then."

"Thank you."

Felicia burst into the sitting room through the entrance room doors just as Ginger came from the dining room.

"Ginger!" Felicia said sounding rather worked up. She didn't even take note of Ginger's obtrusive collar. "I've just come from the theatre."

"What's the matter?"

"It's Matthew Haines. He's missing now, too."

Ginger gawked. "What do you mean, he's missing?"

"Just like Angus. Just gone! No one has seen him. He didn't show up for our auditions. Geordie Atkins called at Matthew's flat, and he wasn't there either. Ginger, someone is stealing actors!"

185

*G*inger settled back in her chair. She couldn't wait to fall into a blissful state of nothingness in the comfort of her own bed.

"Felicia, darling, I don't think anyone is stealing actors. Please tell me what has happened?"

"It's just like with Angus. Matthew and I made plans to meet for lunch before the auditions, and he didn't show up. Of course, I was put out, but I assumed he'd lost track of time. When he didn't show up for the auditions either, I just knew something terrible had happened. Ginger, what have you got around your neck?"

Ginger grinned at Felicia's sudden change of track. "I'm afraid the Daimler and I got caught on a slippery patch of sleet and smashed into another motorcar."

"Are you okay?"

"Yes. A bit of neck strain. I'll be fine in no time."

"What about the Daimler?"

"In the mechanic's garage. I haven't yet heard how it's faring."

"Oh dear," Felicia said. "How unfortunate. But what to do about Matthew?"

How like Felicia to dart back to her own troubles.

"A second missing actor is indeed odd. Then again, perhaps he was inspired by Mr. Green to live in a carefree fashion."

"I just can't believe it," Felicia huffed.

Unfortunately, Ginger could. Mr. Haines didn't seem the type to take much seriously. To placate Felicia, she said, "I'll call Basil and inform him."

"Thank you." Felicia sniffed into her handkerchief then helped herself to a tuna triangle.

Ginger eased to the hall, not moving her head or neck in the slightest. She bent her knees to reach for the candlestick phone and dialled the Yard.

"I'm sorry, madam. Chief Inspector Reed is unavailable."

"Very well, I'd like to report a missing person. Potentially missing." Ginger relayed the information she'd gleaned from Felicia. "This is the second young man from the Abbott Theatre to disappear. It may be purely coincidental. However, it may also be a case where two young men—I'm referring to Mr. Haines and Mr. Green—are in trouble. Please ensure the appropriate investigator is informed."

Ginger returned to Felicia who looked quite forlorn and exhausted.

"Why don't you have a lie down before dinner?" Ginger said gently. "I've let the police know about Matthew. Let's let them worry about it for now."

Felicia yawned into her hand. "I think I shall, Ginger.

Thank you."

Ginger slid back into her chair, exhausted herself. It had been quite a day already, first with the countess's strange performance, then the motorcar accident, then Smithwick's inexplicable visit, and now another missing man.

Why *had* Smithwick bothered to come? If the British secret service was involved, wouldn't Smithwick want her to stay out of the investigation? He never made mention of any desire of that sort. Perhaps it was because they really weren't involved, as Smithwick had implied. If not, then who? The Germans? The Russians? The Romanians?

And why stage it at her gala?

With her foot, Ginger removed the folded easel paper she'd tucked under her chair. Despite the collar, her neck was still sensitive to movement. She rang the bell, and Pippins arrived soon afterwards.

"Pips, would you mind so much?" She poked the paper with her toe. "I need it tacked to the easel again."

"Certainly, madam." Pippins did as requested. "Anything else you need from me?"

"Perhaps some tea."

After adding a log to the fire, Pippins left Ginger alone in the sitting room. She stared at the board.

Lady Ilsa Lyon, *kleptomaniac;* husband Lord Lyon, *protective;* Princess Sophia, *territorial enemies*; Lord Whitmore, *British secret service agent*; Countess Andreea Balcescu, *elusive.*

She retrieved a pencil from a drawer in the sideboard. She was about to scratch out Princess Sophia's name, then stopped. Just because she was dead, didn't mean she hadn't killed Mary Parker.

What *motives* did this crew have?

Next to Lady Lyon, she wrote: *theft.* Had Lady Lyon wanted the real blue diamond badly enough to kill for it? It was hard to imagine her breaking the victim's neck.

Lord Lyon: *defending family name.* It was quite likely that Mary Parker saw her attacker. Ginger could see how he might kill her to prevent his wife from going to court. He was certainly strong enough.

Princess Sophia: Was she working for the Germans to intercept the coded message? If so she had failed. Perhaps she was also after the necklace. Had Mary Parker been wearing the real blue diamond at the gala? Had Sophia merely planted the doubt by telling Ginger it was a fake, waiting until the end of the night to break the lady's neck and switch the necklaces?

Ginger wrote *"theft"* beside the princess' name.

Beside Lord Whitmore, Ginger wrote: *fulfilling his mission?* Perhaps Mary hadn't hung her shawl up with a message inside. Perhaps she was *waiting* for a message to be delivered. Had Lord Whitmore needed to prevent Mary from receiving a message from the Russians? If so, who was the Russian?

Countess Balcescu: *Wild Card*

Lizzie arrived with a tea tray. "Here you are, madam. Would you like me to pour? Perhaps it's better if you sit down."

Ginger slowly lowered herself into a chair and accepted the hot tea. "Thank you, Lizzie."

"Just ring the bell if you need anything else."

"I will."

Ginger blew on the tea to cool it as she stared at the board. The whole thing made Ginger's headache worsen with a vague dizziness. She was still no closer to the truth than she had been this morning. She took a small sip.

"You look like you could use something stronger than tea."

Ginger slowly turned towards Haley's voice.

"I do believe you are right."

Haley's gaze fell to Ginger's neck. "Oh, honey. What happened?"

Ginger relayed her misadventure once again.

"I'm glad it was a minor crash. You'd be surprised how many fatalities involve automobiles." She paused. "Are you in pain?"

"Somewhat," Ginger admitted.

Haley opened her handbag, pulled out a glass bottle of aspirin, and uncorked it. "Take this. It's aspirin."

"Thank you, Haley." Ginger washed the aspirin down with a gulp of tea.

"It was the sleet. We were all travelling at very slow speed. It was a slippery patch—one could barely see it."

Ginger enjoyed the time she and Haley spent together at the end of their days, telling their stories to each other over a short tumbler of brandy. Haley took a moment to stoke the fire, adding another log to keep the flames burning, before pouring two glasses. She handed one glass to Ginger, and they curled up on their respective chairs. Boss must've heard their voices, as he sauntered in and jumped up on Ginger's lap. She stroked his soft fur.

Haley glanced across the room. "I see the chart is back up. What's the new scribble?"

"I'm trying to determine motive. The whole thing is so convoluted."

"Countess Balcescu is a wild card?"

"The countess came to the shop this morning and nosed around upstairs. At first I thought she was interested in the factory dresses, but she acted strangely upon leaving and I followed her."

"Oh, dear."

"If only I had been a second earlier, if I hadn't slipped and torn my best stockings, I would've made the train."

"And then what?"

"I'd know if she actually went to Brown's Hotel, as she said."

"Why would she lie?"

"Because I don't think she's really who she says she is."

"Oh my. Another secret agent?"

"I have no idea. But there was something . . ."

"What?"

"I caught sight of her in the rain, and her face, looked —" Ginger paused, searching for the right words.

"Looked like what?"

Ginger lifted her gaze and wrinkled her nose. "Looked like it was coming off."

Haley considered her statement, then said, "It must've been a refraction of the light in her reflection."

Ginger sipped her brandy. "You're probably right."

CHAPTER TWENTY-FIVE

*G*inger did as the doctor ordered and stayed at home for the next three days. Madame Roux was an absolute darling and fully competent to run Feathers & Flair. Ginger wondered why she bothered going in to assist at all. She was grateful she could lie about in her bed and sleep. She had been more weary than she'd thought.

On the fourth day, Ginger was startled awake by Lizzie in the early morning hours. She leaned up on one elbow, feeling noticeably better. "What is it, Lizzie?"

Lizzie placed an oil lamp on her bedside table. "I'm so sorry to disturb you, madam, but there's a call for you from Scotland Yard. Says it's urgent. I wasn't sure what to do, but I thought you'd want me to wake you."

"You did the right thing, Lizzie." Ginger pushed herself up into a sitting position. "Hand me the bottle of aspirin and a glass of water, will you?"

Her maid did as she was asked. Boss, sensing his

mistress's physical distress, padded softly along the quilt to her side, nudging her arm with his wet nose.

"I'm all right, Boss," Ginger said as she scratched around his pointy ears. "Just need to warm up a little."

Ginger swallowed the pills and then removed the collar and tested her mobility. Much better than the day before. She replaced the collar, accepting that it would be prudent to continue wearing it, but perhaps by the next evening her neck would be strong enough to attend the dance without such an unsightly accessory.

the chief inspector was on the phone? Her curiosity was piqued. Ginger pulled on her dressing gown and took the steps as fast as she could. Boss, her constant companion of late, followed right behind. What could Basil possibly want? The bell-shaped handpiece of the candlestick telephone had been laid on the table on its side. She picked up both pieces.

"This is Lady Gold."

"Ginger, it's Basil."

"Did you find the murderer?"

"Sadly, no. I'm afraid I have a bit of bad news, though."

Ginger thought about the members of her family and was fairly certain all were still in their beds. Almost certain. She could never tell with Felicia—with her increasingly wild ways.

"What is it?"

"It's Feathers & Flair. It's been broken into."

Ginger's jaw dropped. Relieved that it was only her shop and not a loved one in trouble, she was still stunned by the news. Why would someone break into her shop? Her mind could barely comprehend such a thing.

"How badly?"

"The front window is smashed, and everything is thrown about. A constable on patrol saw the perpetrator running away, but couldn't catch up with him in time. Would you like me to fetch you? We need you to identify what, if anything, has been taken."

"Why are *you* there? You don't normally attend to burglaries."

"Feathers & Flair is the scene of an unsolved murder. Shall I come for you?"

Ginger longed for the comfort Basil Reed had brought to her in the past. She couldn't trust her emotions and still wasn't ready to be alone in close quarters with him. She was about to say she'd drive herself when she remembered that her car was being repaired. Dash it!

"That would be kind of you."

Ginger hung up and sought out her maid. "Lizzie, I need to look presentable, and we only have twenty minutes."

Ginger tried to rush up the stairs, but quick movements were uncomfortable. Boss yipped once with glee finding the game exciting, shooting past his mistress and her maid. He stared at Ginger and Lizzie from the landing. His brown eyes glistened with the joy of having won the race.

Lizzie opened the doors of the wardrobe. "A suit, madam?"

Ginger was pleased with her maid's sensibilities. "That would be perfect."

Lizzie presented a brown mid-length wool skirt, a white floral long-sleeved rayon blouse, and a matching tangerine fine-knit scarf. Minutes later, Ginger stood in front of her long mirror examining the look. "It'll do."

Positioning herself in front of her dressing table, Ginger applied a small amount of mascara and a circle of rouge to each cheek. This is what she always did, she rationalised. After all, she rarely left the house without a touch of makeup—she ignored the truth that hammered at the back of her brain—all this effort was because of a particular Chief Inspector soon to be knocking on her door.

Satisfied with the look of her face, Ginger patted her hair and frowned. "No time to fix this, I'm afraid."

"Thank goodness for hats," Lizzie said. She removed a hatbox and presented a tan cloche hat with a broad black ribbon on one side. Ginger smiled. "Well done!"

As soon as they got to the entrance hall, there was a knock on the door. Pippins appeared looking surprised at Ginger's apparent early departure.

She explained as he answered the door. "There's been a situation at my shop that I must attend to."

Basil tipped his hat to Ginger. "Lady Gold."

"I'm ready," she said. "Bossy, you have to stay. If you're good, I'm sure Lizzie will take you for a walk."

The dog sat, looking deflated and sad.

"Come on, Boss," Lizzie said. Boss's disappointment was short-lived as he traipsed happily after the maid.

London streets were quiet before sunrise with only bakers and deliverymen up and about.

"I apologise for dragging you out of bed," Basil said, breaking the silence between them. "Especially with your neck . . ."

"The collar makes it look worse than it is," Ginger said. "I'm feeling much better."

"I'm glad to hear it."

Ginger cast a sideways glance at Basil. He looked tired, his skin was pale, and dark half-moons deepened his eyes. Then she faced him straight on.

"Why did you join the police force? I know it's not because you need a job."

He spoke without looking at her. "So I could bring justice to the marginalised and victimised."

"But why? Everyone says they want justice for the world. What *really* drew you to join?"

Basil slowed the motorcar and held Ginger's eyes. "You know, in all the years I've been married to Emelia, she's never asked me that question."

Ginger glanced away, embarrassed that Basil had compared her to his wife.

She spoke to his reflection in her window. "Are you going to answer me?"

"I had an adopted brother who was murdered when he was five. He was smothered in his bed on a night the nanny was off duty."

Ginger's gloved hand flew to her mouth. Her heart clenched at the horror. "Oh, Basil!" She stared at his profile. The muscle in Basil's jaw twitched but he didn't look her way.

"That's terrible," Ginger said. "Did they find who did it?"

Basil swallowed and shook his head. "No. They didn't really try."

"Why not?"

"Because Elias was black. My father brought him home from South Africa after the second Boer war. He'd been orphaned during the battle."

"Are you sure that's the reason the murderer wasn't apprehended?"

"I understand the law, Ginger, and I know they skewed the evidence."

"How awful!"

"The peerage didn't like one of theirs having a black son," Basil said. "It was simply unconscionable in their minds. They let my parents know how they felt too. But we loved him. He was such a sweet soul."

Ginger pinched her eyes together, disheartened by the prejudice in the system and broken-hearted for Basil. "I'm sorry."

"It was a long time ago."

Basil parked in front of Feathers & Flair and Ginger gasped at the sight of the broken window. Fragments of glass covered the pavement. A police officer stood watching and greeted Basil when he approached. Ginger pulled the door handle of the motorcar, but Basil was there to help her out before she could push it open. He offered her his hand, and she took it. Her neck still complained with too much physical effort.

Inside the shop, Ginger's jaw grew slack. Mannequins lay disconcertingly on the marble floor with dismembered limbs and broken necks. Dress racks had been toppled, and hats dumped out of boxes and crushed. The electric lights shone starkly in the pre-dawn darkness, creating sharp shadows around the wreckage. The effect was sinister.

A quick look upstairs confirmed that the intruder had ransacked the upper level as well.

"I'm sorry this has happened to you, Ginger," Basil said gently.

"What on earth were they looking for?"

"Could it have been a robbery?" Basil asked. There was a slim chance that this crime was an isolated event not connected to the murder, but Ginger didn't believe it.

After a cursory check, Ginger said, "The most expensive gowns are still in the store. The cash box is unmolested, as well. So clearly, he wasn't after money." Not that there was much to be had. Madame Roux only left a float for the next day, always making a deposit at the bank on her way home.

Basil pulled his lips together. "He must have been looking for the cigarette paper."

Ginger's thoughts went to Lord Whitmore. Smithwick had wanted her to believe he hadn't been involved, which was precisely why she suspected him. She lowered her voice. "Could it have been Lord Whitmore?"

"The man who escaped was described as short and stocky. I would describe Lord Whitmore as tall and lean."

"It would be hard to say for sure in the dark of night, would it not? It can be difficult to get a proper perspective."

"Quite."

"The secret service again," Ginger muttered. "Too bad the Yard and MI5 can't find a proper way to work together."

"My men have been through to dust for fingerprints,"

Basil said, "but I would be surprised if whoever did this hadn't worn gloves."

Ginger agreed. Without a strong witness, it would be quite impossible to catch the perpetrator, unless he, or *she* had left evidence behind, which perpetrators usually did. "There must be some clue here," Ginger said. Now that the initial shock had waned, Ginger did a more thorough search. Basil joined her, using a small torch in his quest to find even the slightest clue. Standing behind the cash counter, Ginger stared at the shelves. Something had changed, but her mind couldn't quite pull up what it was. There were rolls of paper for the cash register, paper bags, and folded cardboard boxes to wrap up purchases. A few lost and found items. A leather glove. A change purse. Two scarves.

That was it! When Countess Balcescu had dropped her powder-blue woollen scarf, Ginger had folded it and had put it on that pile. It was gone!

"Basil?"

The chief inspector approached. "Have you found something?"

"It's what I haven't found." She told him about the countess's scarf. "Could the man the constable saw running away actually have been a lady wearing trousers?" Ginger had learned firsthand, that despite the countess's full-figure, she knew how to run.

"It's possible," Basil admitted. "Do you think the countess would go to this trouble just to find a scarf?"

Ginger wrinkled her nose. "Perhaps the scarf was a secondary motive."

"You think she was after the cigarette paper?"

"Well, she failed to find it last time," Ginger said. "It would be a good motive for returning."

Basil scratched his temples. Ginger thought the grey hair growing there made the chief inspector look distinguished. Appealing. She couldn't believe that when they'd first met, she'd thought him too old for her.

Boss, Boss, Boss!

She shook her head to clear that train of thought. Pain shot through the tight muscles of her neck. She grabbed at it and winced.

"Are you all right?"

"Yes. Sometimes I forget about my neck injury."

Basil's warm eyes widened with concern. "I can take you home."

"No, I'm fine.

Basil and most of the constables left with one remaining as a precaution. Ginger was prepared to spend the entire day at the shop, organising the cleaning up, salvaging what could be saved, and counting what couldn't as a loss.

Madame Roux, Dorothy, and Emma were sufficiently shocked and affronted when they arrived.

"*C'est scandaleux!*" Madame Roux immediately picked up the telephone and re-engaged the women who'd helped with the cleaning up after the gala. Once again, Ginger was grateful to her shop manager and appreciated that she knew how to take charge of an unpleasant situation. Before long, everyone had a task, and the cleanup was swift.

Felicia even dropped in to help, a rare moment of self-lessness that Ginger took as a good sign that her sister-in-law was growing up. Ginger ordered a new window and sighed at being told it would take a week to create and install. An ugly sheet of plywood would have to do in the meantime.

"I know what we can do about that," Felicia said.

"Oh?" Ginger responded.

Felicia slipped into her jacket, bundled up with her scarf and gloves, and declared, "I'll be back!" before disappearing out of the door.

An hour later, Felicia returned with a man at her elbow. Ginger hoped it wasn't yet another of her sister-in-law's gentleman friends.

"This is Henri," Felicia announced. "He's a painter."

"Ah, a Frenchman," Madame Roux said approvingly.

"He paints the backdrops for the plays and is really quite fabulous." Felicia gushed at the blushing young man. "He's agreed to paint a mural on the board over the window."

Ginger applauded. "What a brilliant idea!"

CHAPTER TWENTY-SIX

*G*inger could hardly believe the dance was upon her already. At Haley's insistence, she'd spent most of the day resting and her neck felt much stronger than it had the day before. She was happy to take some time away from the neck brace. Even thinking about it made her neck itch.

Lizzie had offered to assist, but Ginger enjoyed getting herself ready. She even started up the gramophone and hummed along to Bessie Smith's *Downhearted Blues*, the lyrics somewhat fitting how she currently felt about Basil Reed. The warm tones of the blues instruments filled the space, getting her in the mood for the dancing yet to come. Perhaps she could allow herself one dance.

She deliberated between several gowns and settled on a chiffon negligee dress and a metallic lace coat. The purple tones worked well with the colour of her hair and the green of her eyes. She'd brought home a new ostrich feather boa from the shop which she wrapped around her neck, and delighted in its softness.

It was a little extravagant for a church dance, but people looked to her to flaunt the latest in modern fashion.

In keeping with the Egyptian craze, Ginger added a tight-fitting turban hat, curling the tips of her red bob with her fingers until they sat nicely on her cheeks. She completed her look with black satin silk shoes decorated with diamanté clasps.

Boss watched from his spot at the foot of the bed as Ginger did a slow turn in front of her long mirror. "What do you think, Boss? Will it do?"

His stub of a tail wagged and he yipped once.

Ginger laughed at her little pet. "I'm glad you like it."

She made up her face using dark shadows and two layers of mascara for her eyes, a sharp eyebrow pencil creating strong arcs, generous spots of rouge on her cheekbones and dark red lipstick for her lips. As she worked, her mind played with the puzzle of the code on the cigarette paper. Decoding encryption was one of the things she had done during the war. Back then, she would focus on nothing else, barely stopping to eat or sleep, until the code was solved. Now, she was juggling too many things to give it enough time.

Ginger paused after clipping on her emerald earrings. It had to be an alphabet/number substitution. There weren't any vowels. She had memorised it once, but since her accident she was no longer sure if she had it right. She reached for the handbag where she'd placed the copy of the cigarette paper, but it was gone. Then she remembered she'd left it in the study.

Boss jumped off the bed and followed her out. She

passed Grace in the passage that led to the late Mr. Hartigan's study. The maid dipped and said, "Madam."

Ginger found her handbag on the desk where she'd left it. Pulling out the small, folded piece of paper, she opened it up and stared.

Boss climbed up on the chair which was pushed up close to the desk. With his hind legs planted on the seat pad, he pressed on the typewriter keys with his paws. Another person might've scolded their pet for being mischievous, but Ginger broke into a smile.

"Boss! You are a genius!"

Ginger positioned herself behind the desk and claimed her father's office chair. "You don't mind, do you?" Boss jumped onto one of the chairs facing the desk and watched excitedly.

She drew the Underwood typewriter closer and placed her fingertips on the home row of keys. Resting her index fingers on the "F" and the "J" she typed out the code.

W533o 8h 849h 975 wt90 @$

She then lowered her fingers one row, her index fingers on the "V" and the "M" then typed the code again, as if her fingers were still on the home row.

STEEK IN IRON OUT SGOP WR

That didn't make sense. Was something meant to be ironed out?

Returning her fingers first to the home row, Ginger then moved them up one row and tried again.

STEEL IN IRON OUT STOP 24

"Steel in. Iron out. 24." She stared at Boss. "Do you know what that means?"

Boss, thrilled to be included in the solving of the puzzle wiggled his small body and let out a small bark.

"I think you're right, but I hope not," Ginger said solemnly. If her guess was correct, someone at MI5 would want to know about the translation. She snapped the sheet of paper out of the typewriter, and went directly to the telephone in the hall to dial Scotland Yard.

A gruff voice answered.

"Chief Inspector Reed," Ginger said. "It's important."

"The chief inspector's out. Can I take a message?"

"Please ask him to call me as soon as he can." Even though Basil had her number, Mallowan 1355, she left it with the officer just in case.

Ginger dialled Basil's home number. She'd rarely called him there, only that time when they were planning dinner together, and she needed to confirm what she would wear for the occasion.

It rang twice before *she* answered. "Mayfair 4459."

"Is the chief inspector there, please?" Ginger said, pushing away the feelings of loss she felt when she heard the lady answer Basil's line. "This is Lady Gold. Is the chief inspector there?"

Though they both behaved the way proper ladies should, there was no denying an invisible barrier lay between them. They both loved the same man, only Ginger had no right to him.

Oh, dear. Did she just admit to being in love? She swallowed hard.

Emelia Reed broke her rambling thought. "I'm afraid he's not yet home from work."

Where was he? Had he gone for a drink instead of straight home to his wife?

"It's important that I speak to him. Please tell him I'll be at St. George's Anglican Church, City of London."

Emelia Reed's voice grew cooler. "Can I take a message?"

"I'm afraid not." It involved the British secret service, so Ginger certainly wasn't at liberty to say. "Tell him I got the message. He'll know what I mean. Please, it's urgent."

"I will," Emelia Reed answered coolly. "Good evening, Lady Gold."

Ginger had made it to the landing on the second floor when the doorbell sounded. Moments later Pippins tapped on her bedroom door. "Reverend Hill is here for you, madam."

"Show him into the sitting room, Pips. I'll be right down."

Ginger selected a gold embroidered handbag from her collection. She paused in front of her chest of drawers before opening the top drawer. She might be going to church, but something told her she could be in need of some assistance. She shifted aside her undergarments and retrieved a small, silver-handled Remington derringer pistol.

CHAPTER TWENTY-SEVEN

*D*ressed in a black shirt and trousers with the distinctive white collar of a vicar, Oliver Hill's cheeks grew rosy when he saw Ginger.

"You look lovely." He produced a small bouquet of tiger lilies, solidifying Ginger's fear that Oliver did consider this something of a date. Perhaps Felicia and Ambrosia were acting as chaperones without any of them realising it.

"Oliver, they're beautiful, but you really shouldn't have."

"One of my parishioners grows them year-round in her conservatory. They are splendid, are they not?"

"Indeed." Ginger called for Grace who, as Ginger instructed, carried the blooms to the morning room. She explained to Oliver, "We get the best light this time of year through the French windows there."

Ginger called up the staircase. "Felicia, darling. Our carriage has arrived. Please check on Grandmother."

There was a quiet moment as Ginger waited with

Oliver, awkward in their silence, each stumbling for something to say.

"Nice of the rain to stop," Oliver finally said.

"I won't have to bring my umbrella."

"No." He waved his palms. "Free hands."

"I hope you have a good turnout."

"You mustn't ever feel a need to make light of your role in helping to start the Child Wellness Project. Many children would be going to bed hungry if not for you." Oliver beamed at Ginger with admiration. If she were the proud type, her feathers would all be on display.

Felicia and Ambrosia eventually made their way down, Felicia dressed in a dropped-waist yellow chiffon dress with narrow sleeves and a six-inch fringe that made the hem look as though it ended lower on the leg than it did. Ambrosia wore a silk tangerine gown with long bell sleeves and a hemline that actually showed a bit of ankle, almost slipping the lady into the twentieth century.

The dowager greeted the vicar with much ado.

"Such a wonderful thing you do for the community, Reverend. I attend my local parish as much as I can, however, the cold weather is not to my liking. Perhaps one day, with spring approaching, Ginger can take me along to St. George's. I would be interested to hear your sermon."

"You're always welcome at St. George's, milady."

Pippins produced long, woollen winter coats for all the women and he and Oliver assisted in helping them put them on.

"Your feather boa is smashing," Felicia said to Ginger. "Is it new?"

"Yes. Only arrived last week. The feathers are ostrich."

Oliver Hill was a competent driver, and Ginger noted that not one horn was blasted in his direction during the whole journey across the city. Impressive.

People were already arriving at St. George's when Reverend Hill's motorcar pulled up.

"The band's quite good, you see," Oliver explained. "Real American Jazz. Too bad you're unable to dance, Lady Gold."

"Actually, my neck feels much better. I'm probably okay for one or two, as long as they're slow."

"Splendid news! I hope you'll save one of them for me."

"Of course."

The parish hall was simply decorated. Ribbon-dotted banners declared the charity name and well-situated candles created a golden glow. As Ginger had predicted, the attendees were mostly working-class members of St. George's Church, doing their bit to help the less fortunate. There was a handful of those who, like herself, found it easy to cross classes. Ginger was pleased to see her staff members supporting the cause. Dorothy, Emma, and Madame Roux were seated together at one table. Even Lord and Lady Whitmore had made an appearance.

Lady Meredith's presence surprised Ginger. Somehow the poor girl had escaped the clutches of her mother. Ginger did hope the girl would be asked to dance.

"Ooh," Felicia cooed. "Look at all the handsome men waiting to dance!"

Ginger smiled at Felicia's enthusiasm, yet her comment concerned Ginger. Felicia had suffered many hardships in her young life. When Ginger had lost her husband Daniel, Felicia in turn had lost her brother. Even though the siblings were seven years apart, they had grown very close after a carriage accident killed their parents. Felicia was left alone to be brought up by her widowed grandmother. Ginger didn't blame her sister-in-law for trying to forget her pain by throwing herself into this new, *laissez-faire* approach to life that young women of the day were enjoying. She just worried that Felicia might one day take it too far.

"I reserved that table for us," Oliver glanced at an empty table near the stage on the far left of the hall. He assisted Ginger out of her coat, then gathered Felicia's and Ambrosia's in his arms. "Mrs. Davies is sitting with us. I'm not sure where she is at the moment."

Probably masterfully making sure the event ran smoothly, Ginger assumed. She needed to remember to send her a gift as a thank-you.

The brass band played a collection of hits from the turn of the century, numbers from the New Orleans Rhythm Kings, Savoy Orpheans, and the Wolverines.

Felicia shouted over the music. "They're pretty good!"

Ambrosia blew her lips as if she held an imaginary trumpet to them. "Much too busy and loud if you ask me."

There was a refreshment table of finger foods and non-alcoholic drinks at the back of the room.

"Do you see a waiter, Ginger?" Ambrosia said. "I'm about to die of thirst."

"I believe you help yourself."

Ambrosia tucked in her chin and leaned over her walking stick. "Help oneself? Whoever heard of such a thing!"

"It's a charity event, Grandmother."

Felicia jumped to her feet. "I'll get us drinks."

She left before deliberation could take place. Ambrosia turned, mouth agape, unhappy that she hadn't been given time to respond. "If only I had a fraction of the energy that girl has."

Ginger saw the motive for Felicia's sudden altruism. An attractive man stood at the refreshment table alone. It wasn't long before Felicia had engaged him in conversation. The gentleman assisted her with the drinks, delivering them along with a plate of bonbons and cakes.

"Thank you, Felicia," Ginger said with a knowing wink.

"This is Mr. Rogers," Felicia said brightly. "He's about to ask me to dance."

The young man stared at Felicia in surprise, smiled, and offered his arm.

Ambrosia couldn't hide her dismay. "A young lady would never have coerced a gentleman into asking her to dance in my day."

Ginger sipped her lemonade as she searched the faces of the attendees. She was pleased by the turnout. And pleased even more to see Lady Meredith on the floor dancing with a gentleman. He was shorter in stature but a match on the dance floor. Good for Lady Meredith! She ought to get out without her mother more often.

Ginger scanned the room back and forth and didn't spot Basil. Evidently, his wife had yet to pass on Ginger's message. The copy of the code and its decryption was folded and buried deep in her dress pocket, and she fingered it for reassurance.

Dorothy West came to Ginger's table, a beverage in hand and looking rather nervous. "Hello, Lady Gold."

"Hello, Dorothy. So nice to see you here."

"Yes. Um, is this seat taken?" Dorothy pointed to the one unclaimed chair.

"No. Please do join us."

Dorothy wasn't the talkative sort. She sipped her drink as her eyes fixated on something across the room. Ginger followed her gaze and raised an eyebrow. Her employee's point of interest was none other than Oliver Hill.

Dorothy caught Ginger's look and blushed. "Reverend Hill is quite fetching for a vicar, isn't he Lady Gold?"

Ginger blinked. Was Dorothy soft on Oliver? The possibility stirred up strange emotions in Ginger. It shamed her to realise she felt possessive of Oliver's affections, even if she wasn't ready to return them.

"Quite fetching, indeed," Ginger replied.

Dorothy leaned in. "You don't live in his parish district, do you? I don't see you here on Sunday mornings."

"I attend a church closer to home when I can." Though Ginger thought, it might be time for a change.

"Then how did you meet Reverend Hill?"

Ginger felt Dorothy's questions quite impertinent. It was hardly her employee's business. However, Ginger remembered how it was to be young and infatuated. In the immature, propriety could be usurped by one's obsession.

Ginger answered, "We have a mutual friend." She smiled softly at the thought of young Scout and hoped that he was warm and safe this night.

Oliver returned, taking his chair with a bound of energy. "Sorry it took me so long," he said. "It can be difficult for me to cross a room without having to stop for a chat with every parishioner I run into."

"How wonderful to be so openly esteemed," Ginger said.

Oliver chuckled. "One does like to be appreciated."

Ginger smiled in return. "One does."

Dorothy watched the interaction, wide-eyed and stone-faced. Noticing her sitting stiffly on the other side of the table, Oliver said, "Hello, Miss West. I'm happy that you've come."

Dorothy's eyes brightened. "You are?"

"Of course. I do hope you will spare me a dance."

If Dorothy had a tail, Ginger thought, it would be wagging. "I will. I will!"

"Splendid," Oliver turned his attention back to Ginger. Ginger suspected that Reverend Oliver Hill had no idea how his simple act of kindness was undoubtedly being misinterpreted by Miss Dorothy West.

Ginger's eyes moved from Oliver's face to a new arrival. She'd been watching for Haley who'd promised to come after her medical school assignment. Instead of Haley, it was a man arriving alone. Black hair parted and combed away from the face, cleanly shaven, a rather prominent nose. His blue eyes were inquisitive, and after paying the suggested donation, he strutted to the edge of the dance floor and looked on with a sly confident smile. His gaze scanned the room for a moment, then locked eyes with Ginger. She quickly looked away.

"Do you know that man?" Ginger said to Oliver.

Oliver twisted his body to see who Ginger was referring to. "With the black hair?"

"Yes."

He shook his head. "No, I can't say I do."

Ginger's attention was captured by Felicia dancing with yet another gentleman. He'd removed his jacket, and had rolled up the sleeves of his white shirt. Like many of the other gentlemen present, he wore a bow tie, and braces (what they called suspenders back in Boston) on his trousers which were just short enough to reveal argyle socks in leather shoes. They were kicking their legs and swinging each other around the room.

"Looks fun," Oliver said.

"A little too physical for me," Ginger said, touching her neck.

The band understood the need to mix slower numbers with the quick steps to give the dancers a chance to catch their breath. A waltz slowed the dancers.

Oliver looked at Ginger expectantly. "Shall we?"

Ginger smiled and stood as Oliver pulled her chair from the table. He took her hand—his was smooth and unexpectedly strong—and led her to the dance floor. Snapping into position, his right elbow went up, left hand stretched out. Ginger giggled at his eagerness and stepped in. She put her hand in Oliver's and placed the other on his shoulder, as he lightly gripped her waist.

He expertly guided her around the dance floor.

"Oliver, you astonish me!" Ginger said when they returned to their table.

"Because I can dance?"

"Because you dance *well*. Anyone can dance."

"You're not so bad yourself, Ginger. Is your neck okay? I hope it didn't prove to be too strenuous."

"I'm quite fine, I assure you."

Haley showed up soon afterwards with Dr. Gupta in tow. Ginger held in her surprise.

"I was bragging to him about the work you and the reverend were doing," Haley said, "and he wanted to come."

Ginger extended her hand. "Good to see you again, Dr. Gupta."

"I'm interested in your work. Perhaps I could offer to do a free clinic for the children."

"That would be fantastic. It's been on my mind to provide more assistance to the less fortunate than simply filling their stomachs. Here, let me introduce you to Reverend Hill."

Oliver was pleased to hear about Dr. Gupta's offer, and they were soon engaged in an expressive conversation of what was obviously a shared passion.

"Looks like our dates have abandoned us," Haley said wryly.

"So Dr. Gupta *is* a date."

Haley scoffed. "Hardly. Merely a figure of speech."

The dark-haired gentleman who'd arrived earlier approached Ginger for the next dance. Ginger half-expected the request as she'd noted his eyes often looking in her direction.

"If no one else is in line, ma'am," he said. His accent was American, from the south.

"You don't mind," Ginger said to Haley, not wanting to leave her to stand alone and give her an excuse to cling to her self-proclaimed wallflower status.

Haley waved her on good-naturedly. "Have fun!"

Ginger had never met the man who now held her hand and her waist in his hands, yet something about him was vaguely familiar.

"I lived in Boston for twenty years," Ginger said as they swayed across the floor. "My stepmother and half-sister still live there."

"Boston's a beautiful city. I'm from a small town just outside of Dallas."

"What brings you to London?"

The stranger's mouth pulled up into a smile, yet his eyes remained cool. "You, actually."

Ginger stiffened. Had this man been following her? All the way from the United States? "I'm sorry, I didn't catch your name?"

The man had positioned them at the edge of the dance floor the whole time. He pulled Ginger close and danced her into a darkened corner. He gripped tightly pulling her so close she couldn't help but smell his cologne. Her heart stopped. She *knew* this scent.

The killer had been in front of her the whole time. She pulled back. "It was *you*."

"Excuse me?"

The countess, Matthew Haines, the Indian laundry boy—*this* man, they were one in the same.

"Mr. Haines? You truly are a master of disguise."

"You're too clever for your own good, Lady Gold."

No wonder Basil and his constables couldn't find a hotel with Countess Balcescu on the registry or any trace of her after she'd disappeared on the train. She didn't exist.

Matthew gripped her hand tightly. Ginger winced. Her gaze went to her handbag hanging from the back of her chair, fifteen feet away. Her revolver would be of no use to her.

"My real name doesn't matter," Matthew said. "You have something I want, and you'll give it to me, or you'll end up as dead as Mary Parker.

CHAPTER TWENTY-EIGHT

"You made a very convincing lady, Mr. *Whoever-you-are*," Ginger said scornfully. "If not an attractive one."

"Vanity is not important to me. Only results." Matthew dropped his phoney American accent and a distinctive Russian lilt formed his words.

"What is it that you think I have?" Ginger asked.

"A coded message. It was planted upstairs in your fancy shop by the treasonous *Olga Pavlovna*, for one of your agents to retrieve. It was my mission to dispose of the traitor and intercept the message."

Mary Parker had arrived late to the gala at Feathers & Flair. She had sneaked upstairs unnoticed to hide her own shawl amongst the new supply, probably when Princess Sophia or Lady Whitmore had captured the attention of the room with their vapours. Not once did Ginger see Lord Whitmore and the grand duchess together. They were very careful not to be associated with each other. Because Lady Whitmore had grown ill, it was impossible for Lord Whitmore to do the pick up without drawing attention to himself. Matthew must have assumed the message was hidden on Mary Parker's person and had killed her before finding out she'd already made the drop.

This explained why Lady Whitmore had made her surreptitious trip upstairs later that week—she was on her husband's errand. No wonder she seemed distraught, leaving as she did without finding what she was looking for.

"What makes you think I have it?"

"Because, Lady Gold, I know about you. I've no doubt that you've found it, read it and have already decoded it. What I don't know is if you've shared your findings."

"I haven't. You know I wouldn't put anyone I cared about in danger by confiding in them."

"They trained you well."

Well enough that Ginger knew the Russian wouldn't let her live once he had the code.

"It's not here."

"I don't believe you."

"Why would I bring it with me?"

"You wouldn't risk someone else finding it. A burglar, perhaps."

The Russian's hands slowly roamed over Ginger's body.

"Do you mind!" Ginger said, jerking back.

He tugged her close again, his free hand slipping into her dress pocket. Ginger twisted, keeping his fingers from gripping the paper. She couldn't let him see the message and get away.

"Don't be coy, Lady Gold. You'll give me the code now.

I'm leaving either way. If I go empty-handed, I'm afraid
something terrible might happen to your delightful sister-
in-law. She's quite a good actress, I have to say, though I
fear her pitiful emotional performance for that cad Green
wasn't an act."

Ginger looked over the man's shoulder to where
Felicia was chatting with Haley at their table, both
unaware of the danger in their midst.

Matthew stuffed his hand in her pocket. Ginger
tensed.

Then suddenly, Matthew was on the ground, palms
covering his face, groaning loudly. "The bounder's broken
my nose!"

Ginger looked at his attacker with amazement.
"Oliver!"

Oliver Hill did a little jig as he cupped his fist, trying to
shake off the pain. "Ow, that hurt."

Matthew writhed on the floor.

"Oh, dear Lord!" Oliver froze to the spot. "I don't
know what came over me."

When Matthew removed his hands from his face,
Oliver gasped at the blood. "I broke his nose clean off!"

"It's a prosthesis, Oliver," Ginger said. "He's not
harmed terribly."

Matthew groaned, his real nose bleeding as he peeled
away the fake. Ginger raced to her handbag and whipped
out the Remington.

"Ginger?" Haley said.

Ginger didn't have time to explain. Ambrosia's
demanding voice called after her, *"Georgia? What on earth!"*

Matthew tried to stay the bleeding with the tails of his shirt as he stumbled to get to his feet.

"Stay down!" Ginger stood with legs braced wide, elbows locked.

"What's this?" Matthew fell back to the floor and smirked. "A female with a pistol?"

"I grew up in America, Mr. Haines. If I fire, I won't miss."

A crowd had formed and Haley and Dr. Gupta pushed their way through.

"What happened?" Haley asked.

"Oliver punched him in the nose," Ginger explained.

Haley cast a questioning glance at the reverend, and he shrugged. "He was behaving in an ungentlemanly manner."

"Dr. Gupta, your tie," Ginger said. "This man is wanted by the police."

Dr. Gupta unknotted his tie and Ginger instructed the Russian to put his hands behind his back. Dr. Gupta tied his wrists.

"Ginger?"

Ginger turned to see Basil Reed in the circle. "I only just got your message. What's going on?"

"Hello, Chief Inspector," Ginger said as she lowered her gun. "This is your killer."

CHAPTER TWENTY-NINE

he constables arrived and escorted a disgruntled "Matthew Haines" to a holding cell.

"Well, wasn't that exciting," Oliver said with a clap of his hands. "What's proper protocol now? Do I need to send everyone on their way?"

"No need to end the dance prematurely, Reverend," Basil said.

Oliver smiled. "Jolly good."

Ginger rubbed the back of her neck. Matthew had been less than gentle, and his rough handling had caused her to jar her neck. She was sure she'd get a talking-to from Dr. Longden.

"Are you all right?" Basil said, noticing her discomfort.

"I'm afraid I have a rather nasty headache."

"Please," Basil said, "allow me to take you home."

"I've had enough excitement myself," Ambrosia said. "Reverend Hill, would you please get me my coat."

"And mine as well," Ginger said. "The chief inspector

has offered to take the dowager Lady Gold and me home early. Would you mind bringing Felicia and Haley later on?"

Oliver's eyes flickered to Basil, and a brief look of uncertainty flashed behind them before he answered. "Yes, of course."

"You're looking pale, Ginger," Haley said. "Perhaps I should return early as well and help you retire."

"I'm quite fine to get myself ready for bed. Besides, I have Lizzie."

"That's right. I always forget you have a maid."

Ginger snorted. Haley forgot nothing. She just liked to rub in her opinion of high society.

Ginger caught Haley eyeing Dr. Gupta, the real reason Haley wasn't insisting she return home to care for Ginger. It wasn't because Haley loved to dance, that was for sure.

Oliver returned with Ginger's and Ambrosia's coats.

"Thank you for coming to my aid tonight, Oliver," Ginger said. She gave him a quick hug. His face flushed a crimson colour.

"I'm just thankful to the Lord that a disaster was averted."

GINGER NEEDN'T HAVE WORRIED about filling dead spaces in conversation with Basil in the motorcar. Ambrosia did a fine job asking him questions about his job and informing him of her opinions about the changing times. When they arrived at Hartigan House, Ginger felt it only polite to invite him in for a nightcap so he could recover from the inquisition.

"A drink, to discuss tonight's events?" she said.

Basil hesitated, and Ginger thought he would refuse her offer.

He looked at her as he turned off the engine of his motorcar. "Okay."

Ginger was determined to act as though this moment was nothing more than what it was—a simple discussion. She asked Lizzie to bring her an aspirin and then sat in front of the fire while Pippins poured them drinks.

"Thank you, Pips," Ginger said. "That will be all for tonight. And tell Lizzie she may retire, as well."

"Do you mind if I use your telephone?" Basil asked.

Was he going to ring his wife? And tell her what? That he was having an evening drink with another lady?

Ginger wasn't about to ask. "Of course," she said. "You know where it is."

Boss, having heard Ginger's arrival, nosed his way into the sitting room and nudged her leg. Ginger patted her lap allowing her pet to jump up. He curled up and closed his eyes as she stroked his soft forehead.

Basil returned, sat, and sipped his gin and tonic. "I called in the decryption to Scotland Yard, and they'll pass it on to the appropriate people at MI5." He raised his glass. "Nice work decrypting it."

"Thank you. Does it mean what I think it means?"

Basil relaxed into his chair and crossed his legs. "What do you think it means?"

"Steel in. Iron out. 24. Stalin in. Lenin out. Twenty-four—hours? I think it means Joseph Stalin plans to kill Vladimir Lenin and become Russia's next dictator."

"Twenty-four hours is long past since that message was supposed to be received," Basil said.

"The twenty-fourth, then."

Basil moved his head side to side as he considered this. "Lenin is already ill. Why not let nature take its course?"

"Perhaps Stalin is impatient," Ginger said. "There are others like Trotsky waiting in the wings. And rumour has it that Lenin was trying to get Stalin removed from his position as General Secretary. Stalin might not be willing to take the chance that Lenin succeeds."

"If true, there would be no way to prove it. Not from here."

"You're right," Ginger conceded. "It probably means something else entirely. It's quite possible that Lenin will rally. He's only fifty-four."

"Whatever the case may be, it was Mary Parker's assignment to let MI5 know."

"She worked for the British side?"

Basil nodded.

For the next while, neither of them spoke. The clock's ticking on the mantel seemed especially loud.

Basil moved to the hearth, stoked the fire with agitated strikes, then spun to face Ginger. He looked wretched.

"I'm not certain I'm doing the right thing."

Ginger tensed at the sudden change in subject. "What do you mean?" Her question was a decoy. Her intuition told her she knew exactly what it meant. Her heart beat heavily in her chest as she awaited his answer.

"With Emelia . . . and you."

"Basil."

"You must know how I feel about you, Ginger. Ever

since the *Rosa* I've been captivated by you. Try as I might, I push away thoughts of you, but my own mind betrays me. Just tell me there is no chance for us, and I'll never bring it up again."

"How dreadfully unfair! You're placing the burden of your marriage on my shoulders."

Basil ran his fingers through his hair, grabbed at the back of his neck. "You're right. I'm sorry."

Ginger's voice dropped. "Do you love Emelia?"

This was the moment of truth, the time for him to admit that his love for his wife had died when she left him for another lover. He thought he'd be strong enough to rekindle their love, but he found he didn't want to. He realised that staying with Emelia would end in bitter unhappiness for each of them.

Basil hesitated, then said, "Yes. I guess I love you both."

It was a declaration of love, but not the kind Ginger could accept. Her heart ached with the knowledge that Basil cared for her, but his professed love for his wife painfully ripped away any hope of happiness together.

"Say something," he pleaded softly.

"You loved her first. And you entered into the sacrament of marriage together. It's no small thing, Basil. I know."

"But Lord Gold never . . ."

Cheated.

"He died. It's far worse."

LATER THAT NIGHT, Ginger opened the drawer of the bedside table beside her bed and removed a framed photograph. She wiped the glass surface with the sleeve of her silk dressing gown. Two months ago, she'd thought she might be able to move on, that she might say goodbye to her lieutenant, Daniel, Lord Gold. But she was wrong. It was too hard.

She kissed the black and white image.

"Love, I've missed you."

Reclining on the bed against her big feather pillows, she held the frame to her chest, closed her eyes, and fell asleep.

CHAPTER THIRTY

*G*inger enjoyed Saturday morning brunches at Hartigan House. Mrs. Beasley always did her best to amaze them with her cooking—fried eggs and bacon, toast slathered in fresh butter, canned peaches, fried kippers and hot tea. Even Felicia roused herself out of bed by ten o'clock to join them.

"I still can't believe that the Countess Balcescu was Matthew Haines all along," Felicia said with a pout. She arrived at the breakfast table in the morning room wrapped in a satin dressing gown. Her short dark hair, yet to encounter a brush, stuck up at the back. "I have the worst luck with men!"

"Good thing none of them is here to witness this display," Ambrosia said with a contemptuous flick of her hand. "Could you not do us the simple courtesy of dressing?"

"I'm only going to go back to bed after this, Grandmama."

Ambrosia huffed but held her tongue. Some battles weren't worth fighting, at least not before breakfast.

"You can't fault Mr. Haines's acting abilities, though," Haley said. Her long curly hair had been left in a loose ponytail down her back, out of her usual faux bob. She, however, had dressed in a casual wool skirt and cotton blouse. "I never recognised him at the dance."

An arsenal of costumes and props had been discovered in Matthew Haines's flat, including a fake dirty-blond moustache he used when playing the actor, and a female down-filled body suit he used to create the countess' figure. Basil had told her during a strictly professional courtesy call that Haines had confessed to working for a pro-Stalin faction of the Red Army. British secret agent Mary Parker had wormed her way into the same circle. No doubt her beauty gave her easy access.

"Mr. Haines had me fooled too," Ginger said. "Without his spectacles or the moustache, and with black shoe polish in his hair—and that *nose*—he looked, acted and sounded completely unlike his actor persona."

Haley chuckled. "Poor Oliver thought he'd broken his nose right off."

"I thought Oliver quite chivalrous," Ginger said.

Felicia agreed. "I wish a man would come to my defence in such a heroic fashion."

"Mr. Haines was quite a master at altering his voice, as well," Haley added. "So unfortunate that he chose to use his talents for ill."

"He confessed to adding chloral hydrate to Princess Sophia's and Lady Whitmore's drinks to create a distraction," Ginger explained.

"A sleeping draught," Haley said. "That would explain why the ladies felt faint."

"Yes," Ginger said. "It's why no one saw him go behind the curtain into the changing rooms with Mary Parker."

"Such a scoundrel!" Ambrosia blustered.

"I'm just glad it's over," Ginger said. "The man we know as Matthew Haines will hang for his crimes."

Boss whimpered at Ginger's side and when he'd got her attention, Ginger slipped him a piece of bacon.

Lizzie arrived with a fresh pot of tea and refilled everyone's cups.

"Shall I take Boss for his morning walk, madam?" she asked of Ginger.

"If you don't mind. I have work to attend to after this."

Lizzie left with Boss just as Pippins entered with the Saturday paper.

"News from Russia, madam. I thought you'd be interested."

"Thank you, Pips." Ginger took the folded newspaper and spread it open on the tabletop.

LENIN DEAD AT 54. Lenin's body lies in state in Moscow.
Red Military dictatorship possible.

Ginger stared straight ahead, unseeing. Did Vladimir Lenin die of a stroke as reported? Or had he, as the coded message had suggested, been murdered?

She shared a look with Haley who was now reading the article. Other than Basil, Haley was the only other person Ginger had told about the coded message.

The cigarette paper and the decoded message had

been delivered through Scotland Yard to MI5. Apparently, Mary Parker had overheard murderous plans from the pro-Stalin faction of the Red Army hinting at Stalin's plan to expedite his leadership in Russia. Ginger didn't know what England could do with this news except to be prepared for more Russian refugees. Hopefully, Europe wouldn't be drawn into another war.

"Did they ever find out who the *Blue Desire* belonged to?" Felicia asked.

"Yes," Ginger said, refilling her tea. "A baroness from Lithuania. There was a jewel theft at a bank there, and the blue diamond was stolen. It changed hands along the way, and apparently a number of people died along the way too. Eventually, Princess Sophia came into possession of it. No one knows how exactly, and sadly she can no longer tell us. She had a paste made as a precaution, knowing the diamond had a history of getting stolen and a reputation for being unlucky. Indeed, her paste had been stolen.

According to Mr. Haines's confession, Princess Sophia let the 'countess' in on the little secret at the gala after having one too many glasses of champagne."

"Mr. Haines was a busy fellow," Haley said.

"Yes. Once he had his eye on the *Blue Desire*, his original assignment became second priority. He dressed as a laundry boy to steal the diamond. Princess Sophia startled him in the act of searching her room and he killed her."

"That *is* unlucky," Haley said with a straight face.

"How did Mary Parker come to have the paste of the blue diamond," Felicia asked.

"Eventually the stolen paste made it back to Russia

where Mary Parker somehow came to be in possession of it," Ginger said. "Even the fake is unlucky it seems."

"My goodness," Ambrosia said. "What a convoluted tale."

"I wonder if I should get pastes made of my valuable jewels," Felicia said as she stood to go. Ambrosia followed after her.

"What valuable jewels do you have, Felicia? Don't tell me you've been receiving expensive gifts from these young men you entertain."

"Oh, Grandmama. I jest."

Ginger couldn't help but laugh after them. "They're quite a pair."

Haley agreed. "They are." She pushed away from the table. "I have to go back to the school." She twisted her ponytail and expertly pinned it up into a faux bob with hairpins she'd stored in her pocket. She'd done it so often she evidently didn't even need a mirror. Ginger was impressed.

"On a Saturday?" Ginger asked.

"A delivery of cadavers is due to arrive at the mortuary." Haley's dark eyes flashed with anticipation, and Ginger had to smile. Only Haley would show so much enthusiasm over something so macabre.

"Well, have fun," Ginger said. She finished her tea and headed for the study where work she'd ignored with all the excitement over the last week was piled high. A letter awaited her, lying benignly on a silver platter on the desk. Using the letter opener, she sliced the envelope open. There was one sheet of thin paper folded inside.

. . .

Dear Mrs. Gold,

It was fun, wasn't it? I thought I'd set the exchange in your shop, to entice you. Just admit it, you want back in the team again.

Yours sincerely,
Captain Francis Smithwick

GINGER HUFFED as a sharp anger filled her. Captain Smithwick had purposely used her gala for his dirty work. She would never again put herself in a position of weak subordination to another person and especially not to that man. Fuming, she struck one of her father's matches, lit the letter, and tossed it into the hearth.

"Enough," Ginger muttered aloud. "I shan't waste another second thinking about that man."

She returned to her desk and sorted through invoices and order forms. She opened the accounting ledger she'd brought home from Feathers & Flair and perused the income and expense columns. She was happy to note that despite the ghastly murder, her shop had done well over the last week. This was good news for the Child Wellness Project as Ginger funnelled a good amount of the proceeds there. In fact, Ginger had plans to see Oliver later that afternoon. He said it was to discuss the charity and how they'd proceed. Ginger hoped that was all the reverend wanted. She thought she'd made her position clear, but experience had shown her that sometimes the message doesn't get through the first time.

Every so often Ginger had to rest her head. Dr. Longden had encouraged her to take it easy. Warm baths and a good sleep did her neck wonders, but it would be a couple of weeks before it would be healed.

Pippins tapped on the door, and Ginger welcomed him inside. "Miss Higgins is on the telephone for you, madam." Ginger made a mental note to have a new telephone installed in her office as she pushed away from her desk. She'd call the telephone company immediately after talking to Haley.

"Hello, Haley."

"I have something to tell you, and it's not good news."

Ginger tensed. "What is it?"

"Dr. Watts ordered two cadavers which were delivered to the medical school last night, and this morning there were three in the freezer. One more than there should be. One that isn't registered."

"How odd." Ginger wondered what this news could have to do with her.

"Ginger, I think I found your missing man."

"My missing man?"

"Felicia's friend, the actor."

"Angus Green?" With all the kerfuffle over Mary Parker and Princess Sophia, Ginger had nearly forgotten about the missing man. "He's dead?"

"Yes. He's been murdered."

Ginger grabbed at the string of beads around her neck. *Oh, mercy.*

The End.

IF YOU ENJOYED READING *Murder at Feathers & Flair* please help others enjoy it too.

- **Recommend it:** Help others find the book by recommending it to friends, readers' groups, discussion boards and by suggesting it to your local library.
- **Review it:** Please tell other readers why you liked this book by reviewing it on Amazon or Goodreads. If you do write a review, let me know at **leestraussbooks@gmail.com** so I can thank you.
- **Suggest it** to your local librarian.

This book has been edited and proofed, but typos are like little gremlins that like to sneak in when we're not looking. If you spot a typo, please report it to: **admin@leestraussbooks.com**

SIGN up for Lee's readers list and gain access to Ginger Gold's private Journal. Find out about Ginger's Life before the SS Rosa and how she became the woman she has. This is a fluid document that will cover her romance with her late husband Daniel, her time serving in the British secret service during World War One, and beyond. Includes a recipe for Dark Dutch Chocolate Cake!

http://www. leestraussbooks.com/gingergoldjournalsignup/

DON'T MISS *Murder at the Mortuary!*

Read on for an excerpt!

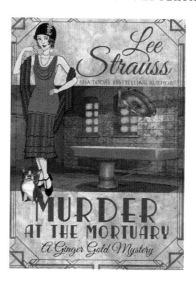

Cadavers can be deadly . . .

UNREGISTERED CORPSES ARE SHOWING up amongst the cadavers in the mortuary of the London School of Medicine for Women. Unnatural deaths. Murders. The first known victim is recognized by Haley Higgins, a third-year pathology student. War-widow fashionista Ginger Gold feels a responsibility for the man's death and is determined to find his killer.

Her pursuit takes her into the dangerous realm of the famous Italian gangster Charles "Derby" Sabini. With the help of Haley and the handsome Chief Inspector Reed - an uneasy alliance - Ginger investigates shady dealings at the docks and at the racehorse stables. What does one have to do with the other, and how are they connected to the bodies piling up at the mortuary?

Someone is working on the inside at the school, and Ginger has to find out who before she, or someone she loves, ends up lifeless on a ceramic mortuary slab.

www.leestraussbooks.com

Get your copy at Amazon or order from your favorite book store.
Read on for chapter one.

VISIT LA PLUME PRESS TO SEE FULL CATALOGUE

www.laplumepress.com

Volume 3

HIGGINS & HAWKE MYSTERY SERIES

(cozy 1930s historical)

The 1930s meets Rizzoli & Isles in this friendship depression era cozy mystery series.

Death at the Tavern

Death on the Tower

Death on Hanover

THE ROSA REED MYSTERIES

(1950s cozy historical)

Murder at High Tide

Murder on the Boardwalk

Murder at the Bomb Shelter

Murder on Location

A NURSERY RHYME MYSTERY SERIES(mystery/sci fi)

Marlow finds himself teamed up with intelligent and savvy Sage Farrell, a girl so far out of his league he feels blinded in her presence - literally - damned glasses! Together they work to find the identity of @gingerbreadman. Can they stop the killer before he strikes again?

Gingerbread Man

Life Is but a Dream

Hickory Dickory Dock

Twinkle Little Star

THE PERCEPTION TRILOGY (YA dystopian mystery)

*Zoe Vanderveen is a GAP—a genetically altered person. She lives in
the security of a walled city on prime water-front property along side
other equally beautiful people with extended life spans. Her brother
Liam is missing. Noah Brody, a boy on the outside, is the only one who
can help ~ but can she trust him?*

Perception

Volition

Contrition

LIGHT & LOVE (sweet romance)

*Set in the dazzling charm of Europe, follow Katja, Gabriella, Eva,
Anna and Belle as they find strength, hope and love.*

Sing me a Love Song

Your Love is Sweet

In Light of Us

Lying in Starlight

PLAYING WITH MATCHES (WW2 history/romance)

*A sobering but hopeful journey about how one young Germany boy
copes with the war and propaganda. Based on true events.*

A Piece of Blue String (companion short story)

THE CLOCKWISE COLLECTION (YA time travel romance)

Casey Donovan has issues: hair, height and uncontrollable trips to the 19th century! And now this ~ she's accidentally taken Nate Mackenzie, the cutest boy in the school, back in time. Awkward.

Clockwise

Clockwiser

Like Clockwork

Counter Clockwise

Clockwork Crazy

Clocked (companion novella)

<u>Standalones</u>

As Elle Lee Strauss

Seaweed

Love, Tink

ABOUT THE AUTHOR

Lee Strauss is a USA TODAY bestselling author of The Ginger Gold Mysteries series, The Higgins & Hawke Mystery series, The Rosa Reed Mystery series (cozy historical mysteries), A Nursery Rhyme Mystery series (mystery suspense), The Perception series (young adult dystopian), The Light & Love series (sweet romance), The Clockwise Collection (YA time travel romance), and young adult historical fiction with over a million books read. She has titles published in German, Spanish and Korean, and a growing audio library.

When Lee's not writing or reading she likes to cycle, hike, and stare at the ocean. She loves to drink caffè lattes and red wines in exotic places, and eat dark chocolate anywhere.

For more info on books by Lee Strauss and her social media links, visit leestraussbooks.com. To make sure you don't miss the next new release, be sure to sign up for her readers' list!

Did you know you can follow your favourite authors on Bookbub? If you subscribe to Bookbub — (and if you don't, why don't you? - They'll send you daily emails alerting you to sales and new releases on just the kind of books you like to read!) — follow me to make sure you don't miss the next Ginger Gold Mystery!

www.leestraussbooks.com
leestraussbooks@gmail.com

MURDER AT THE MORTUARY

CHAPTER ONE

It was unclear how long Angus Green had been dead.

Ginger Gold studied the postmortem photos laid out on the top of her desk. Before his untimely death, Mr. Green had been a young man with a privileged upbringing. Felicia, Ginger's sister-in-law, had met the chap while acting in the same stage play. It was Felicia who'd begged her to take on the missing person's case. Ginger had agreed and failed.

Ginger glanced around her father's study. *Her* study now. Somehow, Ginger doubted she'd ever get used to calling her father's things her own. Like the furniture. She felt like a little girl sitting in Daddy's huge chair, its springs worn by the weight of her father as he leaned back, propped his leather shoes up on the desktop, and tented his fingers on his chest. Like this, he pondered the deep mysteries of life.

Ginger brought her thoughts back to the mystery in front of her. Not that Ginger professed to be a private investigator, not officially at any rate. It was just something she often found herself doing—perhaps a residue from the secret service work she had done during the Great War. Some things are hard to unlearn.

Thinking about Felicia seemed to summon the younger woman's presence because she sauntered into Ginger's study uninvited and possessed an empty chair in front of the desk. Boss, Ginger's black and white Boston terrier, lifted his head from his spot near the hearth to acknowledge her.

Felicia's dark hair, shingled with the fringe pinned back, was in need of washing. Her normally rosy, youthful skin appeared drawn, and shadows were thick under her eyes. "Still nothing?" Unsmiling, Felicia crossed her arms and her legs and stared at Ginger.

Ginger sighed. "Some cases take longer to solve than others."

"And some never get solved at all," Felicia huffed.

"Unfortunately, that is correct."

A stiff silence stretched between them like barbed-wire.

"I'm sorry I didn't take you seriously when you first came to me," Ginger offered.

"You shouldn't have stopped looking for him."

Ginger swallowed a thick lump. Felicia blamed her—which Ginger thought fair. After all, Ginger blamed herself too. Perhaps, if she hadn't become obsessed with another case, Angus Green would still be alive.

"I know you're angry with me," Ginger said. "Though Haley says it's quite possible that Angus was killed before you'd even learned he was missing."

Haley Higgins, a dear friend and long-term guest at

Ginger's home, Hartigan House, was a student of forensic pathology at the medical school. She'd provided Ginger with copies of the photographs of Mr. Green's body, now scattered over the top of the desk.

"Of course, she'd say that," Felicia replied tersely. "She's your friend. She's defending you." Without giving Ginger a chance to respond, Felicia sprang to her feet and stormed out of the study. Boss whimpered.

Ginger ran long manicured fingers through her red bob and inhaled. She hadn't saved Angus Green's life, but she could bring his killer to justice. *She must bring his killer to justice.* She stared at the photos again.

Angus Green on the theatre poster: alive, young, and virile.

Angus Green in the mortuary, lying flat out on a ceramic slab, ghostly white with a deep-red gunshot wound in the centre of his unblemished forehead. Though the photo was black and white, Ginger knew about the colouring of the body—she'd seen it for herself shortly after it was discovered.

London in 1924 wasn't the Wild West. Ordinary citizens didn't own a gun. Ginger, an exception to that rule, found great comfort in carrying her small, silver Remington derringer—a gift from her late husband.

Without the bullet that killed Mr. Green or its shell, it was impossible to determine what type of pistol had been used to carry out the execution. The copy of the post-mortem report signed by Dr. Manu Gupta, interning doctor of forensic pathology, was well worn from frequent handling. Ginger reread it.

Dr. Gupta's report was thorough in its measurements

and weights of all the organs. Despite the bullet's passage between the right and left lobes of the brain, and a corresponding exit wound on the back of Mr. Green's skull, Angus Green had a healthy heart, lungs, kidneys, and spleen. Intestines and lower abdominal regions were average as well. Because the body had already been washed and embalmed before discovery, there was no residue of gunpowder, though the impression of the wound pointed to close range.

Abrasions on the wrist indicated that Angus Green's hands had been tied. Haley, who had assisted Dr. Gupta, had found trace amounts of dark soil under the fingernails. Peculiar since Angus Green had been the posh type of gentleman who kept his nails clean and neatly trimmed.

Lab reports had yet to come in for the soil sample, however, toxicology reports confirmed the presence of cocaine in Mr. Green's blood. It appeared that Angus Green's manner of amusement went beyond the stage. Ginger leaned back, and the old chair nearly gave way on her.

"Deuced chair!" Ginger grabbed her chest. "Nearly gave me a heart attack."

Boss yipped and dashed across the room at the sound of his mistress' distress.

"Oh, Bossy." Ginger scooped him into her arms. "I'm all right, but I appreciate your valour all the same."

The telephone—newly installed, black with a modern square design—rang in deep repetitive tones. Ginger placed Boss on the floor and pushed the offending chair aside.

Ginger answered, "Mallowan 1355."

"Lady Gold?" The caller was female with a French accent.

"Hello, Madame Roux. Is everything all right?" Madame Roux managed Ginger's Regent Street dress shop, Feathers & Flair.

"*Oui, oui.* I am only ringing to inform you that the shipment of fabric from India has arrived. Should I get Emma to sort it, or would you like to have a look at it first?"

Emma Miller was Ginger's in-house designer, and Ginger had every confidence in her. "Tell Emma to go ahead."

"She'll be pleased, madam. She's eager to start sewing."

After saying goodbye, Ginger took another long look at the photos on the desk before heading to the passageway and calling for her longtime butler. "Pippins?"

The ability of Clive Pippins to materialise when beckoned never ceased to amaze Ginger. The kindly man, a septuagenarian with hunched shoulders and translucent skin, had a surprising amount of energy and enthusiasm for life. His eyes remained clear and as blue as cornflowers. They twinkled when his gaze landed on Ginger.

"Madam?"

"Pips, do me a terrific favour and shop for a new office chair for me, please. Father's old chair practically sent me flying."

"Certainly, madam. Is there anything else?"

"Yes. Ask Clement prepare to drive me to the medical school. I shall be ready to leave in thirty minutes. And let Lizzie know she'll be looking after Boss." Lizzie was

Ginger's young maid and an enthusiastic companion of the little Boston terrier.

Ginger checked the time. She had to hurry if she didn't want to be late for the class on trace evidence. She had long since envied Haley for being able to continue her education—an option that had closed for Ginger when she got married—but the administration didn't see a problem with her sitting in, especially once she'd become a financial benefactor of the institution. In fact, Ginger had organised a much-anticipated charity gala for the school that was to take place at the weekend.

The class on trace evidence was held in a medium-sized room with white walls and wooden floors. Situated in the middle was an oak table that sat twelve. A third of the seats were taken, since, according to Haley, only a handful of the senior students were interested in forensic pathology as a career choice. Most of the students were concerned about the living and how to keep them alive. Like Haley, Ginger found forensic science tremendously exciting. She spotted Haley and slipped into the empty seat beside her.

"You made it," Haley said, her American accent coming through.

"Clement drove," Ginger responded by way of explanation. She found the middle-aged man to be an excruciatingly slow and cautious driver, no doubt due to the fact he was inexperienced at driving in the city. He'd only just begun to get the hang of Ginger's old 1913 Daimler before it was damaged in a motorcar crash. She couldn't expect too much from the timid man. A gardener by vocation, he'd come with Ginger's grandmother-in-law when she moved in.

Ginger had expected Dr. Watts—the chief pathologist and college administrator—to teach the class, but instead of the stocky, white-haired man, a younger and slimmer gentleman strode confidently to the front of the room near the end of the table.

"Good afternoon," the man said with a strong Irish lilt. "For those of you who don't know, I'm Dr. Sean Brennan. Since you now know my name, and I've not had the same privilege, please introduce yourselves."

Polite introductions followed:

"Florence Jennings." A no-nonsense type wearing a bland day dress and round spectacles spoke her name softly.

"Matilda Hanson," said a pretty girl with a heart-shaped face and a pouty Clara Bow mouth. In fact, she resembled the famous Hollywood actress with her short brunette curls and her dark, soulful eyes. An unlikely candidate for pathology at first glance, if someone were to judge by looks alone

Next, a middle-aged woman with a stern stare said, "Agatha McPherson."

"Haley Higgins."

"Lady Georgia Gold."

As if startled by Ginger's title, Dr. Brennan blinked with a jerk of his head.

Had he heard of her somehow? Ginger wondered.

"Jolly good," he said, smiling. "Let's crack on, then. I'm thrilled about the advancements in modern forensic science, a valuable study for medical doctors and crime investigators alike. For example, the recent advances in blood grouping not only assists doctors in making a proper diagnosis and giving proper treatment, but our friends at Scotland Yard can use blood analysis to solve crimes. As forensic pathologists, you will work closely with the police. Today, we're going to talk about trace evidence, and how the smallest thing can be a big clue."

Ginger leaned towards Haley and whispered, "Where's Dr. Watts?"

Haley whispered back, "His wife is very ill. He's recently taken leave to be with her."

"I'm sorry to hear that." Ginger liked the elderly man, almost as much as Haley did. Dr. Watts was a highly esteemed forensic pathologist and an excellent mentor to Haley.

Ginger watched Dr. Watts' replacement with interest. He wore a grey wool and cashmere suit with its cuff-bottom trousers. His blond and wavy hair, parted on the side, was oiled back behind small ears. The enthusiasm in his eyes showed his love for teaching, and the lines on his face proved that he smiled often.

"Forensic science is a burgeoning field, and the implications for crime detection and solution are exciting," Dr. Brennan said. "Imagine, a simple fingerprint leading to a conviction. Under the same circumstances in former times, the culprit would've got away with murder."

Dr. Brennan reached into the pocket of his waistcoat and removed a magnifying glass. "Our fictional friend, Sherlock Holmes, is never without one of these." He presented it like a flag. "And neither should you be. Please access yours."

Ginger reached into her handbag and removed a new magnifying glass from its protective velvet bag. She couldn't believe she hadn't procured one before now.

Dr. Brennan held a forefinger in the air. "Turn to the person next to you and compare each of your fingerprints. What pattern do you see? Arches? Whorls? Loops?"

"I already know what mine are," Ginger said. "Do you?"

Haley scoffed. "Of course. My ridges form arches."

Ginger laughed. "And mine, whorls."

Ginger offered her palm and Haley gripped Ginger's fingers, examining each one.

"You are correct," Haley said, offering her fingertips for Ginger's examination.

Ginger studied Haley's ridges under her magnifying glass. "I find it amazing," she said, "that, despite a mere three basic patterns, every single fingerprint is completely unique to its owner."

Haley agreed. "So very unfortunate for the criminals around us."

When the group had completed the task, Dr. Brennan said, "Now, take a look at the fabric of your frock. Examine each fibre and select one in particular. What colour is it? Is it bright and new or faded and worn? Is the texture smooth or rough? Perhaps there is a partial stain —what caused it? Tea? Wine? Blood?

Wanting to blend in with the student body, Ginger's wardrobe choice was a soft pink Coco Chanel with a v-line dropped-waist wool dress trimmed in braids and buttons in the same fabric. She accessorised with a white cloche hat with black ribbons, flesh-coloured silk stockings, and black Mary Jane leather shoes. Under the magnifying glass, the strands of wool looked like earthworms.

"I spilled coffee on my sleeve this morning," Haley said, staring at the spot on her rayon blouse with her magnifying glass. "Even though I thought I'd cleaned it thoroughly with water, under the magnifying glass I can see traces of it remaining."

"Let me see," Ginger said, and Haley extended her arm towards her. Ginger hovered her own glass over the area. "Interesting. What once was hidden, has now been revealed."

Get your copy at Amazon or order from your favorite book store.

ACKNOWLEDGMENTS

Much love to the growing list of fans who have fallen in love with Ginger Gold! You make all the "blood, sweat, and tears," worthwhile.

Once again my editorial/publishing team pulled through: Angelika Offenwanger, Robbi Bryant, Heather Belleguelle, and Shadi Bleiken. Thank you! A special shout-out to Heather for helping me get to the end of this book with something worth publishing. Some books write themselves-this one wasn't one of them!

I'd like to honour Heather's mother, Daphne Finch, an early reader and a fan of the Ginger Gold Mystery Series who passed away during the writing of this book. She'd taken a cue from Ginger and had been heard saying, "*Oh, mercy,*" which I thought was wonderful.

As always, my heart belongs to my family—my husband Norm Strauss, and kids, Joel & Shadi, Levi, Jordan and Tasia. Special thanks and much love to my parents, Gene and Lucille Franke, and my circle, Donna,

Shawn, Noreen and Lori. I'm so grateful for your prayers and practical support.

I must tip my hat to Lisa Lockwood for coming up with the name of Ginger's shop, Feather's & Flair, and to Mark and Coreen Biech for providing the Romanian name Andreea Balcescu.

My eternal gratitude to Jesus who keeps me sane.

Made in the USA
Middletown, DE
21 May 2021